P9-BJS-527

Collectors
FINE ART
OF · HAWAII

Hawaii's Premiere Galleries

PRESENT

Art Touched by Disney Magic

Bring the magic of Disney home with limited-edition sericels from Walt Disney Animation Art.
Each sericel is created using the fine art process of serigraphy to capture
the animated films and characters that have lived in our hearts forever.

"Hawaiian Holidays" size: 12" x 16"

"He Loves Me"
size: 14 3/4" x 15 3/4"

"Little Lady"
size: 8 5/16" x 11 11/16"

Walt Disney
ANIMATION ART

"Winnie the Pooh and Story Time Too"
size: 15 1/4" x 14 1/4"

"Bouncy, Trouncy Tigger"
size: 26" x 9"

© DISNEY. Published by Walt Disney Art Classics

AT THE HYATT REGENCY - KAANAPALI, MAUI
Telephone: 808.661.1032 • Toll Free Nationwide: 800.778.5222 • Facsimile: 808.661.0733

Kauai • The Hyatt Regency Kauai • Tel: 808.742.8331 • Toll Free: 800.786.2787
Kauai Marriott Resort and Beach Club • Tel: 808.246.0928 • Toll Free: 800.679.9797
Kauai Princeville Hotel • Tel: 808.826.1340 • Toll Free: 800.968.7200
Kauai Sheraton Hotel • Tel: 808.742.1225 • Toll Free: 888.449.7749
The Big Island • The J Gallery • at The Orchid • Mauna Lani • Tel: 808.885.0950 • Toll Free: 800.643.1669
California • Gallery Nash • Carmel • Tel: 831.622.9009 • Fax: 831.622.9405

CONTENTS

David B. Fleetham

©T&CO. 2000

TIFFANY & CO.

EACH A PROMISE. "Etoile" diamond engagement rings and wedding bands in platinum and eighteen karat gold.

Maui Whalers Village 808.667.7899

OFFICE OF THE MAYOR

COUNTY OF MAUI
200 SOUTH HIGH STREET
WAILUKU, MAUI, HAWAII 96793

A MESSAGE FROM MAYOR JAMES "KIMO" APANA

Welcome to Maui County. Our beautiful islands, Maui, Molokai, and Lanai, offer an atmosphere of colorful sceneries, tropical climate and friendly people.

You will experience the white sand beaches, waterfalls, natural wonders, historical sights, special events, cultural awareness and accommodating recreational facilities.

Enjoy the Aloha spirit of Maui County as local people refer to our islands as "no ka oi", the best.

Aloha,

JAMES "KIMO" APANA
Mayor, County of Maui

ABOUT THE COVER

"Hawaiian Majesty" by Leonard Wren captures the spirit and captivates the soul. Wren himself is a true "American Impressionist" and has made a striking impact on the world of impressionistic art. The eye travels miles into a Wren painting drawn by the unique technique of layers of paint creating distance and perspective. To learn more about Leonard Wren and view his other works, visit Collectors Fine Art of Hawaii. See page 3 for more information.

CONTRIBUTING PHOTOGRAPHERS

Ron Dahlquist • Dave B. Fleetham
David Glickman • Jacob Maui
Joe Harabin • Randy Hufford
Greg Koob • Chris Wayne
John Severson • Maria Veghte
Steve Brinkman • Ric Noyle

PRODUCTION ASSISTANTS:

Mark Elies • James Yamada

DISTRIBUTION:
Gavin Campbell and Tante Sumibcay

The Best of Maui guidebook is published by Sandwich Islands Publishing Company, Ltd. All rights copyright ©2000 Sandwich Islands Publishing, Ltd., P.O. Box 10669, Lahaina, Maui, Hawaii 96761 (808) 661-8177 • Fax: (808) 661-2715

VISIT US ON THE INTERNET:
www.bestofmauiguide.com

SANDWICH ISLANDS PUBLISHING CO., LTD.

Joan Arnold
Founder

Joseph Harabin
Publisher

J. Douglas Arnold
President

Jamie Arnold
Associate Publisher

Kathy Fruh
Sales/Marketing

Chris Arnold
Vice President

Printed in Singapore by SNP Printing Pte Ltd, 97, Ubi Avenue 4, Singapore 408754 • Tel: 65-7412500 • Fax: 65-7447098

Ultimate Expressions of the Soul

Campanile

YOUR MOVE 40 x 30

AFRICA ON MY MIND 30 x 40

Lahaina Galleries
Hawaii's Fine Art Gallery

PANE FORMAGGIO 12 x 16

MARTINI AFFAIR II 12 x 20

BEFORE DAWN 40 x 30

Meet our artists on Friday evenings as we celebrate
"Friday Night Is Art Night" in Lahaina!

728 Front Street
Lahaina, Maui
(808) 667-2152

The Shops at Kapalua
Kapalua, Maui
(808) 669-0202

The Shops at Wailea
Wailea, Maui
(808) 874-8583

Mauna Lani Bay Hotel
The Big Island
(808) 885-7244

Fashion Island
Newport Beach, California
(949) 721-9117

645 Beach Street
San Francisco
(415) 749-1000

www.lahainagalleries.com • email: lgi@maui.net • 1-800-228-2006

This edition of the Best Of Maui
is dedicated in loving memory
of our founder, mother, wife, and friend
Joan D. Arnold

Maui,

Another day of
powerful beauty
ends with one
last encore.
Photo by Ron
Dahlquist.

*I*N THE BEGINNING, there was Pu'u
Kukui, the now extinct volcano that created what is now West Maui. Then there was
mighty Haleakala, the now dormant volcano
that created East Maui. Then there was an isthmus
connecting the two landmasses, created by matter that
had eroded from the slopes of the opposing volcanoes.

Combined, they form today's Maui, the Valley
Isle, the second-largest island in the Hawaiian chain
at 728.8 square miles.

Contained within Maui's shores are a remarkable variety of settings, a feature that makes man's
recreational pursuits here seem boundless.

Tropical rain forest climb the slopes reaching up from
the windward shores of East Maui. Further up the terrain
turns alpine, where evergreens flourish and enters the lunar
climes of Haleakala Crater, where the island's highest
point, the lookout at Pu'u Ulaula, looms 10,023 feet above
sea level. At this altitude snowfall occurs occasionally.

The western slopes of Haleakala are rugged , des-
olate lava fields and desert lands that would seem
more appropriate to Arizona.

Erosion, brought about by 400 inches of rain
annually, has sculpted sharp peaks and valleys in the

The Island

West Maui mountains, coloring the faces emerald.

Fabulous white sand beaches fringe the west-facing shores where the sun shines most of the year. Lava cliffs rise up from the north shores. Black sand graces some of the beaches eastward, as does red.

Harbors break the reef windward in Kahalui and leeward in Maalaea and Lahaina.

The windswept central valley is carpeted with undulated sugar cane. Also centrally, as well as northerly, fields of pineapple. Tracts of ranchland score the slopes of the volcanoes.

At the northern end of the valley are the business and population centers of Kahului, where the main airport is located, and contiguous Wailuku, the counties seat. At the south end is Maalaea, the little harbor village, and Kihei, a former dessert that now boasts one of the fastest growth rates on the island.

On the shores stretching farthest east is Hana, called "the last Hawaiian place."

This is Paradise, sought out by those seeking pleasure from around the world. With such a variety of elements composing its tapestry, can it be any wonder why Maui has come to be known as "No Ka 'Oi" or simply, "the best."

Maui Ocean Center

The Maui Ocean Center is a celebration of one of the world's most diverse and unique marine environments. Discover all that Maui's underwater tropical paradise has to offer without ever getting wet, or learn what to look for as the perfect introduction to a snorkel or dive trip.

The ocean around the Hawaiian Islands is unique and beautiful, combining a breathtaking world of rugged mountains and valleys, remnants of ancient lava flows and volcanic fields. The tropical marine environment includes spectacular corals, exotic endemic fish, tremendous pelagic sea life, humpback whales, and other marine mammals. The Maui Ocean Center is a state-of-the-art aquarium that brings this intriguing underwater world within easy reach of visitors of all ages.

This unforgettable journey guides you from black lava shorelines and white sandy beaches, descending underwater past live corals and brilliantly colored tropical fish, through lava tubes and sea caves, and deep into the open ocean. Awesome indeed, but you will not be alone on this journey, as there are Naturalists throughout the park to answer your questions and guide you through this adventure.

The Center's walkthrough glass aquarium rooms allow viewing of life among the coral gardens where the State fish, humuhumu-nukunukuapuaa, can be found.

Dozens of innovative exhibits and habitat galleries welcome you as you explore Hawaii's underwater world. Meet eye-to-eye curious garden eels, unusual frogfish and the shy octopus. Marvel as a giant stingray glides by, or feel the smooth spines of a bright orange slate pencil urchin in the Touch Pool.

The Whale Discovery Center pays tribute to the wonder, majesty and mystery of the humpback whale — Hawaii's State Marine Mammal. From the depths of the ocean, you follow a pod of humpback whales halfway around the world as they mate, feed and migrate across the vast Pacific.

Descend into the deep blue and gain a spectacular glimpse of the open ocean. Translucent and delicate jellyfish dance in front of you. Amazing sharks, colorful jacks and spotted eagle rays pass above and below you as you stroll through an acrylic tunnel in the middle of an enormous 750,000-gallon tank.

Linger during your visit and enjoy the warm Maui sun, breathtaking view, and sumptuous Pacific Rim cuisine in the Seascape Ma'alaea Restaurant. For a light lunch, ice cream or refreshing drink, there's the Reef Café.

The Maui Ocean Center Store features exclusive ocean-related jewelry, art, crafts, clothing and books that make this one of Maui's most exciting shopping destinations.

E komo mai... come, explore this spectacular underwater world. Learn rich cultural stories about Hawaii's deep connection to the sea, as you view the grand spectacle of nature just below the waves. For more information, call (808) 270-7000.

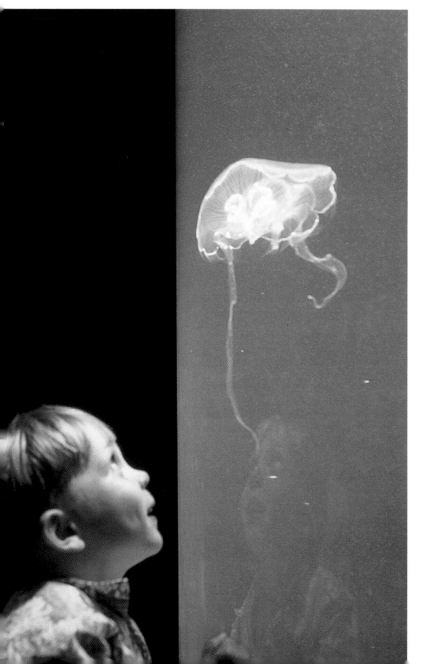

A water tube of transparent Jellyfish exhibit the alien beauty of life in our oceans.

MAUI OCEAN CENTER™

"Maui's Favorite Attraction" as voted by readers of Today Magazine

Hawaii's ultimate ocean experience

- The largest tropical aquarium in the Western Hemisphere
- Spectacular living coral reefs
- Marine life found only in Hawaii
- Interactive Whale Discovery Center
- Ocean experts guide your experience
- Beautiful oceanfront park setting

© David B. Fleetham

The Underwater Journey

Seascape Restaurant

Maui Ocean Center Store

Turtle Lagoon

Whale Discovery Center

MAUI OCEAN CENTER.
The Hawaiian Aquarium

Highway 30 at Maʻalaea Harbor Village, Maui, Hawaiʻi
Open Daily 9 a.m. - 5 p.m. • Phone: (808) 270-7000

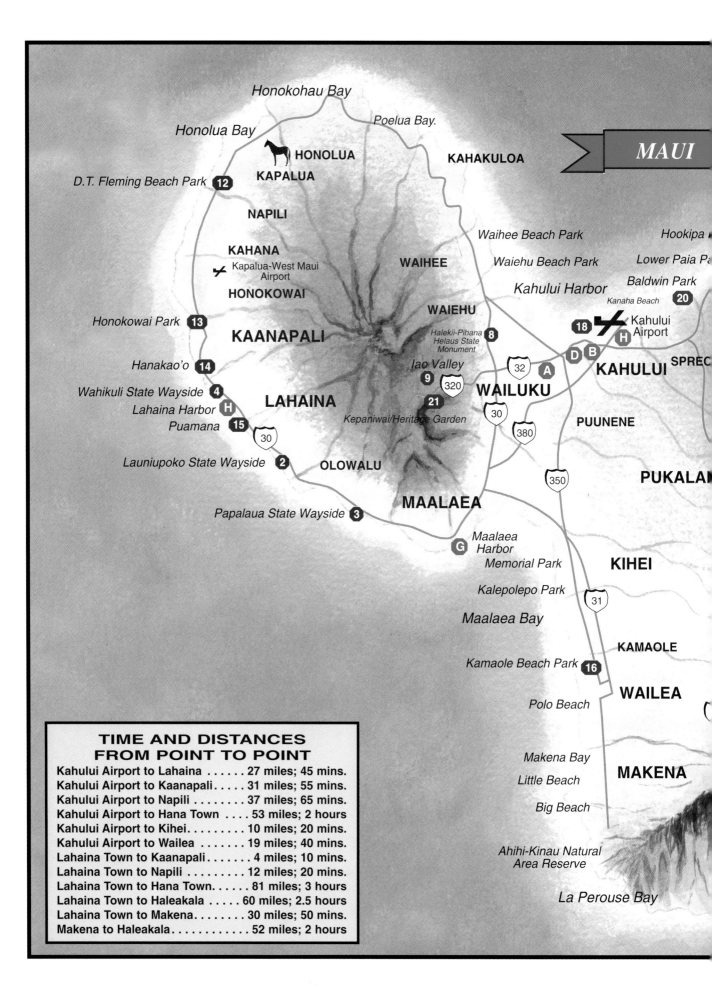

Honokohau Bay

Poelua Bay.

Honolua Bay

HONOLUA

KAHAKULOA

MAUI

KAPALUA

D.T. Fleming Beach Park **12**

NAPILI

Waihee Beach Park

Hookipa

KAHANA

Kapalua-West Maui
Airport

WAIHEE

Waiehu Beach Park

Lower Paia Pa

Baldwin Park

HONOKOWAI

Kahului Harbor

Kanaha Beach **20**

WAIEHU

Honokowai Park **13**

KAANAPALI

Halekii-Pihana
Helaus State
Monument

8

18 Kahului
Airport

H

Hanakao'o **14**

Iao Valley

9 **320**

A

D B

KAHULUI

SPREC

Wahikuli State Wayside **4**

WAILUKU

Lahaina Harbor **H**

LAHAINA

Puamana **15**

30

Kepaniwai/Heritage Garden

32

30

PUUNENE

21

380

PUKALA

Launiupoko State Wayside **2**

OLOWALU

350

Papalaua State Wayside **3**

MAALAEA

KIHEI

G Maalaea
Harbor

Memorial Park

Kalepolepo Park

31

Maalaea Bay

KAMAOLE

Kamaole Beach Park **16**

WAILEA

Polo Beach

Makena Bay

MAKENA

Little Beach

Big Beach

Ahihi-Kinau Natural
Area Reserve

La Perouse Bay

TIME AND DISTANCES
FROM POINT TO POINT

Kahului Airport to Lahaina . . . . . . 27 miles; 45 mins.
Kahului Airport to Kaanapali. . . . . 31 miles; 55 mins.
Kahului Airport to Napili . . . . 37 miles; 65 mins.
Kahului Airport to Hana Town . . . . 53 miles; 2 hours
Kahului Airport to Kihei. . . . . 10 miles; 20 mins.
Kahului Airport to Wailea . . . . 19 miles; 40 mins.
Lahaina Town to Kaanapali. . . . . . . 4 miles; 10 mins.
Lahaina Town to Napili . . . . 12 miles; 20 mins.
Lahaina Town to Hana Town. . . . . . 81 miles; 3 hours
Lahaina Town to Haleakala . . . . . 60 miles; 2.5 hours
Lahaina Town to Makena. . . . . 30 miles; 50 mins.
Makena to Haleakala. . . . . 52 miles; 2 hours

N

SHOPPING

C. Hana Flower Co.
A. Local Motion (Kaahumanu Center)
B. Maui Coffee Roasters (444 Hana Hwy)
D. Roland's Shoes (Maui Mall)

ACTIVITIES

H. Alex Air Helicopter Tours
H. Hawaii Helicopters
F. Maui Cave Adventures (Hana)
G. Maui Ocean Center (Maalaea Harbor)
E. Ohe'o Stables (Kipahulu/Hana)
H. Active Volcano Air Tours (Kahului Airport)

DINING

A. Kaahumanu Center
  • Edo Japan
  • Maui Tacos
  • The Coffee Store
G. Maalaea Harbor
  • The Coffee Store

Park
19
PAUWELA
Waipio Bay

PAIA

HAIKU
KAILUA   HUELO
Honomanu Park
Kaumahina State Wayside
VILLE
11
ALIIMAILE   **KEANAE**
6 *Wailua Valley State Wayside*
360   **WAILUA**
7 *Puaa Kaa State Wayside*
NAHIKU
365

W. Kuiaha

MAKAWAO

Hana   *Waianapanapa*
Airport   *State Park & Cave*
OLINDA   **F**   **5**

377

378   **C**   **17**
                              Hana
37 **KULA**   *Beach*
                    Haleakala National Park   **HANA** *Bay*
10   **1**

Polipoli Spring State
Recreation Area   **KIPAHULU**

ULUPALAKUA   *Seven Pools*
                    E

Four-wheel
drive recommended
31   *Kaapahu*
                    Bay
          KAUPO

TRANSPORTATION SERVICES

SpeediShuttle (see ad on page 59)

**Red Locations refer to
Maui's Parks and Beaches
on pages 16 and 17.**

MAUI'S PARKS AND BEACHES

EXPLORING PARADISE

Maui has national, state and county parks galore for your enjoyment. From the 10,000-foot level of Haleakala National Park to county beach parks at sea level, there is a park on Maui bound to please anyone.

Lower on Haleakala's slopes you can hike through a forest of Redwood trees or hunt sugar plums in Polipoli State Park. Or farther up, explore more than 30 miles of trails through the mighty volcanic crater of the National Park.

Choice beach parks and scenic areas offer camping facilities, but permits are often required so check local rules first. Reservations are also needed for cabins and access to more "primitive" areas.

But there are enough easy-to-get-to public trails winding throughout Maui to keep the most avid trekker busy.

Most county parks are beach parks for day use only with cold showers, fire pits and restrooms.

State parks, meanwhile, include everything from historic sites to wildland areas. Some, such as Polipoli and Waianapanapa, allow free tent camping though again, a permit is usually required.

From the sea to high atop the slopes of Haleakala, Maui is a park-filled recreation paradise.

NATIONAL PARKS

1 HALEAKALA NATIONAL PARK

Includes the summit of the dormant volcano that dominates Maui as well as The Seven Pools area of 'Ohe'o Gulch on the coast beyond Hana. There are three campgrounds, all available free on a first-come, first-served basis, except for cabins in the crater which must be reserved in advance. No permit required at Hosmer Grove campground. No facilities at 'Ohe'o Gulch camping area. Plenty of hiking trails throughout the park and swimming is popular in the lower pools when conditions are safe.

Remember, it will take at least two hours to reach the crater in Haleakala National Park from Kihei or Lahaina and there is no food or gasoline available when you get there. Your last chance to stock up on supplies will be in Pukalani. Summit temperatures are 30 degrees lower than on the beaches. Dress warmly.

The visitor center at the summit, besides a magnificent view of the crater, has exhibits to explain geology, archaeology, and ecology of the park. Admission to the park on the crater road is $3 per vehicle. For daily updates on weather conditions and other park information call (808) 572-7749, otherwise write Haleakala National Park, Box 369, Makawao, HI 96768. (28,000 acres).

Background photo by Dave Fleetham.

HAWAII STATE PARKS

State parks are open year-round. There are no admission, parking, picnicking or camping fees, except for lodging in cabins which must be reserved in advance. For information call (808) 244-4354, or write to the Department of Land and Natural Resources, State Parks Division, P.O. Box 1049, Wailuku, HI 96793.

2 LAUNIUPOKO STATE WAYSIDE

On Honoapiilani Highway (Hwy 30), 3 miles south of Lahaina. A small beach park with swimming, beach activities and picnicking tables, grills, restrooms, children wadding pool. (5.7 acres).

3 PAPALAUA STATE WAYSIDE

On Honoapiilani Highway (Hwy 30), 14 miles southwest of Kahului Airport. A small wooded beach park with swimming, snorkeling, fishing and picnicking. No drinking water. Tables, grills, restrooms. (6.7 acres).

4 WAHIKULI STATE WAYSIDE

On Honoapiilani Highway (Hwy 30), about 2.5 miles north of Lahaina. A small beach park with swimming, sheltered picnic area and beach-related activities. Canoe race site (often referred to as Canoe Beach), showers, restrooms, stoves. (8.3 acres).

5 WAIANAPANAPA STATE PARK

Located off the Hana Highway (Hwy 360), about 52 miles from Kahului. A remote volcanic coastline with cabins, camping area, picnicking, shore fishing and hiking along ancient Hawaiian trails. Features include legendary caves, a heiau, blowholes, natural stone arch and small black sand beach. Reserve cabins and camping in advance. Showers, restrooms. (120 acres).

6 WAILUA VALLEY STATE WAYSIDE

On Hana Highway (Hwy 360), about 32 miles east of Kahului. Excellent views of the Keanae Valley and Koolau Gap in Haleakala's rim, Wailua Village and taro patches. No facilities.

7 PUAA KAA STATE WAYSIDE

On Hana Highway (Hwy 360), about 38 miles east of Kahului. A rest stop and picnic grounds in the rain forest with small waterfalls and pools. No drinking water.

8 HALEKII-PIHANA HEIAUS STATE MONUMENT

In Wailuku at the end of Hea Place, off Kuhio Place from Waiehu Beach Road (Hwy 340). Includes the

The numbers before each park name correspond to the numbers on the Maui map on pages 12-13.

remains of two important temples of worship (heiaus) that were rededicated as war temples by Kahekili, Maui's last ruling chief. Also a good view of Central Maui. (10.2 acres).

9 IAO VALLEY STATE MONUMENT
At the end of Iao Valley Road (Hwy 32), about three miles from Wailuku. Includes spectacular valley scenery and view of the Iao Needle, a 1,200-foot geological feature carved by nature from volcanic rock. Gates open 7 a.m. to 7 p.m. daily. Swimming (natural pools), rest stop. (6.2 acres).

10 POLIPOLI SPRING STATE RECREATION AREA
In the Kula Forest Preserve at the 6,200-foot elevation level, 9.7 miles from Kula on Waipoli Road off Kekaulike Avenue (Hwy 377). Four-wheel drive vehicles recommended. Extensive hiking trails through the fog belt of Southwestern Haleakala - redwoods, cypress sugi, cedar trees, and an understory of ferns and mosses. Camping and one cabin (no showers). Sweeping views of Maui and outer islands in clear weather. Pig and bird hunting in season with license. (10 acres).

11 KAUMAHINA STATE WAYSIDE
On Hana Highway (Hwy 360), about 28 miles east of Kahului. Picnicking, camping (no showers) and scenic views of the northeast Maui coastline. (7.8 acres).

MAUI COUNTY PARKS
Most county parks are beach parks, with picnic facilities, restrooms and showers. Overnight stays require a permit for a nominal fee that can be obtained from the County Parks Department, War Memorial Gym, Baldwin High School, Rm 102, Kaahumanu Avenue (Hwy 32), Wailuku, HI 96793. Call (808) 244-5514.

12 D.T. FLEMING
Located just north of Kapalua on the Lower Honoapiilani Highway. Picnicking, swimming, beach activities, shower/restroom facilities. Great for body boarding.

13 HONOKOWAI
A small rocky beach park with a palm-shaded picnic area and restrooms just north of Kahana on the Lower Honoapiilani Highway.

14 HANAKAO'O
A long sandy beach with swimming, snorkeling and other beach activities, showers and restrooms, on the Honoapililani Highway (Hwy 30) between Lahaina and Kaanapali.

15 PUAMANA
Shaded grassy picnic area with great views of Lanai and Kahoolawe. Rocky beach.

16 KAMAOLE
Three separate beach parks designated I, II and III in Kihei with swimming, beach activities, snorkeling, picnic and restroom facilities. Shopping and dining across the street.

17 HANA BAY
On Keawa Place off Uakea Road in Hana with swim-

ming, snorkeling, beach activities, covered picnic area, restrooms, showers and snack shop.

18 KANAHA BEACH
Located between Kahului and the airport with picnic facilities, swimming and windsurfing. Wide, white sand beach on 1 mile of shoreline. Excellent board sailing site. Restrooms and showers.

19 HO'OKIPA
On Hana Highway (Hwy 36) a few miles past Paia with covered picnic area, restrooms, and showers. One of the best windsurfing beaches in the world. Excellent surfing, but limited swimming and snorkeling due to rough water and strong currents.

20 H.P. BALDWIN
On Hana Highway (Hwy 36) between Kahului and Paia, with swimming and beach activities, camping (with permit), restroom facilities and showers. Most popular beach park on windward Maui. Surf breaks along entire wide white sand beach.

21 KEPANIWAI PARK AND HERITAGE GARDENS
On Iao Valley Road (Hwy 32) between Wailuku and the Iao Needle with picnic pavilions, restroom facilities, and re-creations of Maui's ethnic homes and gardens.

The drive to Hana is long and slow, but the rewards are both dramatic and refreshing. Photo by Ron Dahlquist.

Please help keep Maui clean. Pick up your trash before leaving our parks and beaches.

Timeline of the Sandwich Islands

A CANOE of the SANDWICH ISLANDS, the ROWERS MASKED.

Thousands of ocean-going koa wood canoes were the principle means of travel around the Hawaiian island groups. From original field drawings by John Webber, the official artist on Captain Cook's final voyage. All prints courtesy of Lahaina Printsellers.

Hawaiians had no written language until the 1820s when Western missionaries translated the Hawaiian sounds into English-language phonetic letters. Before this time certain talented elders could recite from extraordinary memory the history or genealogies of their families back to their first arrival.

Circa 500 A.D.
Large ocean canoes carrying perhaps 200 people from Marquesas Islands 1500 miles south of Hawaii settle the Big Island first. Several expeditions made the hazardous trip bringing domestic animals and food plants. They lived 53 generations in which no man was made chief over another.

Circa 1200
A small group from Tahiti arrived. All Hawaiian nobility can trace their origins back 40 generations to this arrival and Pa'ao the first chief to build a heiau, initiate human sacrifice, and kapu laws.

1500s
A royal road, the Alaloa, circles Maui signifying unity

1788
Captain James Cook's third and final voyage with 182 men and two ships set foot in the Islands documenting the existence of the Hawaiian people for Europeans. Gave these islands the name of Sandwich Islands in honor of his English patron the Earl of Sandwich. Modern research indicates perhaps 800,000 people living on the 8 major Hawaiian islands.

1790
Kamehameha of Big Island defeats Maui forces in Battle of Iao Needle, using Western cannon.

1795
Battle of Maui and Oahu. Kamehameha I defeats Maui's king Kalanikupule with 6000 canoe force consolidating his kingdom except Kauai.

CA MORAI, in ATOOI.

Illustration of a Hawaiian heiau on Kauai prepared on Captain Cook's voyage. Heiau are stone platforms where ceremonies to the gods, including human sacrifice, were performed. All aspects of life were dictated by the gods. The kahuna priests interpreted the will of the gods and passed this information to the Chiefs who enforced these interpretations by a series of irreversible decisions, the kapu system. The largest remaining heiau in the Hawaiian islands is accessible through the Kahanu Gardens on the coast near the Hana airport.

1800-
1830 Aromatic Sandalwood trees sold to Asian traders in exchange for Western weapons, clothing, furniture. Hawaii's first export trade. Tree harvested almost to extinction.

1803 First horses introduced, naturally multiplying to an 1884 peak of over 30,000.

1810 Through marriage Kamehameha I receives Kauai ceded by King Kaumualii uniting the entire Kingdom of Hawaii under one ruler, a monarchy which lasted until 1895.

1819 Kamehameha dies. Kapu system abolished by Kamehameha II and his advisors, destruction of heiau temples signal overthrow of the traditional Hawaiian religion. First whaling ships arrive marking rise of Lahaina as whaling capitol.

1820 First permanent Western settlers arrive, 20 missionaries from New Bedford, Massachusetts to begin the great conversion to Christianity.

1826 Hawaiian language standardized with five vowels and seven consonants.

1831 Lahainaluna High school opened, oldest institute of secondary learning West of Rockies, Hawaiian nobility and newly wealthy of California sent children here.

1832 New Testament translated and printed in Hawaiian.

1839 Declaration of Rights — Hawaii's Magna Carta granted protection to the land and property of the people.

1840 Hawaiian Constitution provided for a public school system: English as the medium of instruction.

1843 Hawaiian Islands under British flag due to hasty annexation by a naval captain. Six months later countermanded by British Foreign Office.

1846 Whaling visits to Hawaii peak with 596 arrivals. 429 anchor off Lahaina.

First drawing of Hawaiian people from Cook's voyage. These people, racially pure because of remote location, lived in an idyllic climate and supported themselves by farming on large irrigated terraces and a system of man-made fish ponds.

Priest of Ku god wearing a gourd helmet to keep his psychic powers, or mana, concentrated, and individual identity secret.

1848	Great Mahele. First written records and procedures for land ownership dividing land between kings, chiefs, and commoners.
1850	Legislative act authorized the sale of lands in fee simple to resident aliens. Capitol moved from Lahaina to Honolulu.
1868	First of thousands of Japanese contract workers arrive to work sugar plantations, subsequent migrations of Portuguese, Koreans, Filipinos.
1871	Remaining Hawaiian whaling industry destroyed in Arctic ice jamb; petroleum replaces whale oil.
1875	Reciprocity Treaty with U.S. opened sugar trade and gave plantations a viable U.S. market.
1876	Hamakua Ditch completed as the great irrigation system bringing water from Maui's rainy north shore to the sugar fields of central Maui: Science taming nature to serve men.
1878	Hawaii's first telephone with three miles of line from Haiku to Paia, Maui.
1885	Pure Hawaiian population reduced to 40,000 through 100 year contact with Western viruses. Imported nationalities reinvigorate and mix to produce the vigorous people of Hawaii in modern times.
1887	Bayonet Constitution. King Kalakaua in bloodless revolution agrees to ceremonial status with propertied minority having the real legislative, executive, and judicial power.

Sailors from New England signed on to a hazardous four year round-trip voyage to hunt Pacific whales for an average net pay after expenses of $54. The best museum on Maui devoted to this period can be found in the center of the Whalers Village shopping center, Kaanapali.

1893 Hawaiian Monarch Queen Liliuokalani overthrown by American Republican forces in Honolulu. No casualties.

1894 Hawaii's first auto a Wood electric. To secure a $2 drivers license three things required by examiner. How to start the car, how to keep it going, how to stop it. Speed limit 15 mph in town.

1900 Hawaii becomes territory of the U.S., only 5% of population of American or English ancestry.

1901 Pioneer Inn in Lahaina opens as Maui's first visitor hotel.

1904 First gasoline powered auto in Hawaii, by 1991 100,000 registered vehicles on Maui.

1930s Paia becomes major town on Maui due to sugar boom with many plantation camps grouped by nationality. Lahaina lost importance. Maui a minor agricultural island. Big Five companies dominate.

1935 First regularly scheduled air passenger service from Hawaii to Mainland in 16 hours.

1941 Japanese planes attack U.S. Pacific Fleet at Pearl Harbor, martial law declared.

1959 Hawaii admitted as 50th State.

1962 First hotel built in Kaanapali, the Royal Lahaina Resort, beginning discovery of Maui as major tourist destination.

1974 First non-stop direct Mainland flights to Maui.

1976 Replica of an ancient Polynesian voyaging canoe sailed to Tahiti in 34 days without charts or instruments confirming Hawaiian legends and signaling the rebirth of widespread respect for Hawaiian culture.

1990 Commission established to return Kahoolawe island to civilian control, military bombing suspended. Major Airport Expansion.

1992 18,000 hotel and condominium rooms for 2.2 million annual Maui visitors.

ISLAND WORDS

Just so you know what you're saying!

This short list contains words you might hear on your stay in Maui. Hawaiian is a living language with some elementary schools using it for the principle means of instruction.

The Hawaiian language appears to have only 12 letters. This is because the Hawaiians did not have a written language until the one created by Americans in early 1800s. This first effort neglected to indicate the spaces between some syllables. Proper written Hawaiian needs to have a mark knows as the okina (') included between some vowels to alert where there is actually a minute pause or break in the air stream. Some linguists consider this a true consonant. As one example in English, the glottal stop is the sound you hear between the o's when you say "oh-oh"

The difficulty in pronouncing Hawaiian names as commonly written is that when several vowels are together it is not obvious where the distinct syllable breaks occur without this mark or unless you know common Hawaiian words so as to recognize the word within the word. And as a rule, every word, and every syllable, must end in a vowel.

Hawaiian is a perfect phonetic language and, unlike English, is spelled like it sound. There can be no spelling bees in correctly pronounced Hawaiian – everyone would win.

'aina (eye-na) – land, earth.

aikane (eye-kah-nay) – friend, companion.

akamai (ah-kah-my) – smart.

ali'i (ah-lee-ee) – a chief or member of nobility.

aloha (ah-lo-ha) – hello, goodbye, love.

auwe (ow-way) – an expression or exclamation meaning Oh! or Ouch!

'awa (ah-vah) – root of Piper Nigerum (Kava), a South Seas root, chewed in native Polynesia in a relaxing social ritual.

ea (eh-ah) – sovereignty, rule, life force.

halau (ha-laow) – hula school or troupe.

hale (hah-lay) – house.

hana (hah-na) – work (pau hana=finished with work).

hanai (ha-nai) – adopted or foster children/family. The grandparents often raised the children in traditional Hawaiian families.

haole (ha-oh-lay) – foreigner.

Haoli Makahiki Hou (ha-oh-lee ma-ka-he-key ho) – Happy New Year.

heiau (hay-ee-ow) – ancient temple, place of worship.

holoholo (ho-lo-ho-lo) – to go on a trip or excursion.

hono (ho-no) – bay.

"Best New Show!"
—*Wayne Harada, Honolulu Advertiser*

HAWAI'I REDISCOVERED

There is a wind peculiar to Maui that rises at twilight. It whispers of other places and other times, both mythic and real. The ancient Hawaiian name for this wind is " 'Ulalena." It is also the name of the newest and most amazing stage production to come from Hawai'i in decades.

'Ulalena is a unique and compelling story. And at Maui Myth & Magic Theatre, it is an impressive theatrical experience. The theatre is a multi-million dollar, state-of-the-art venue built for this presentation. It employs the talents of some of Hawaii's most distinguished musicians and performers, combining live traditional Hawaiian music with 8-channel surround sound. Traditional Butoh theatre is blended with acrobatic feats of strength and beauty. Hula is combined with modern dance. Rich costumes, lighting and stage design are woven together into a filagree of fantastic images drawn from Hawaiian legend and history, pulling the viewer out of time and into a place of wonder. Critics agree, 'Ulalena is a feast for the senses and a must see!

Call today for reservations. Two shows nighty, Tuesday - Saturday.
Dinner and Show packages are available at some of Lahaina's finest restaurants.

MAUI MYTH & MAGIC THEATRE PRESENTS

'ulalena

BY ARRA-MONTRIAL

661-9913
878 FRONT STREET, LAHAINA
WWW.MAUITHEATRE.COM

PHOTO CREDIT:
ROBIE PRICE PHOTOGRAPHY

Vacations For This Generation

...and the next

In the 1960's, the average hotel room on Kaanapali Beach was around $30 per night.

Today the same room rents for $100's per night.

At this rate, 30 years from now, the same room could rent for $1,000's per night.

It's your vacation. Own it!

Secure a lifetime of awesome vacations for you and your family today...come discover Vacation Ownership the Embassy way.

Stop by our open house daily 9am-5pm and receive a complimentary poster by:
ROBERT LYN NELSON.
America's most respected marine artist.
(Retail value of $30)

EMBASSY VACATION RESORT®

Kaanapali Beach

(877) 669-MAUI
e-mail: islandescape@sunterra.com

ISLANDS

Maui (mow-wee) – the Demigod that snared the sun.
Lana'i (la-na-ee) – day of conquest.
Molokini (mo-lo-kee-nee) – molo=turn, kini=multitude.

TOWN NAMES

Lahaina (la-hi-na) – tourist literature attributes this to mean "land of the cruel sun", although the older Hawaiian name for this once capital city is "Lele".
Kapalua (ka-pa-loo-ah) – arms embracing the sea.
Nāpili (na-pee-lee) – luck will cling.
Kahana (ka-ha-na) – a district on an island with a stream and valley.
Olowalu (oh-low-wah-loo) – joint action, group.
Ma'alaea (ma-ah-lie-ah) – red color, as earth.
Kīhei (key-hay) – shawl, cape, tapa garment.
Wailea (why-lay-ah) – ocean star.
Kahului (ka-hoo-loo-ee) – athletic contest.
Wailuku (why-loo-koo) – destructive water.
Paia (pa-ee-ah) – clearing in forest.
Ha'ikū (ha-ee-koo) – broken hills.
Pukalani (poo-ka-law-nee) – hole in the heaven (clouds).
Makawao (ma-ka-wow) – view from an island region foreseted, but not precipitous.
Kula (koo-la) – open country, pasture.
Hāna (ha-na) – alert.
Māhinahina (ma-hee-na-hee-na) – pale moonlight.

"KAHUNA"

(kah-hoo-na) — priest, sorcerer (someone who has secret knowledge)
There are several different kinds of kahunas:
La'au lapa'au . . . . . .Herb healer
Lomi lomi . . . . .Healer who uses massage
Ka hea . . . . .Healing at a distance using prayer
Ho'o pono pono . .Heals spirit between people (mediator)
Pule . . . . .Healing by prayer to God
Ha ha . . . . .Diagnosis by touch
Ha'i ha'i . . . . .Sets bones
O'o . . . . .Healing by piercing
Ho'o Hapai . . . . . .Takes care of mother before birth
Ho'o Hanu . . . . . .Midwife
Pa'ao'ao . . . . .Works with small children
'Ana'ana . . . . .Sorcery, uses magic

huhu (hoo-hoo) – angry.
hui (hoo-ee) – club, association, company, partnership.
huna (hoo-na) – secret.
imu (ee-moo) – underground oven.
kama'aina (kah-mah-eye-na) – a person born in, acquainted, or familiar with a place.
kanaka maole (ka-na-ka ma-oh-lay) – the true Hawaiian people.
kane (kah-nay) – man.
kapu (kah-poo) – taboo or sacred, forbidden, no trespassing, keep out.
keiki (kay-kee) – child.
kokua (koh-ku-ah) – help, assistance, donation, as in the sign you often see that says "Please Kokua, no littering (smoking, etc.)".
kuleana (koo-lee-ah-na) – immediate garden or taro patch near a home. One's area or responsibility.
kupuna (koo-poo-nah) – elders, ancestors, grandparents.
lani (lah-nee) – heaven.
lolo (low-low) – crazy or unbalanced.
lua (loo-ah) – bathroom, toilet.
luau (loo-ow) – Hawaiian feast or celebration.
mahalo (mah-ha-lo) – thank you.
makai (ma-kai) – toward the sea.
menehune (meh-nee-hoo-nee) – legendary race of tiny people who worked at night building fish ponds, roads and temples.
mauka (mao-ka) – inland, toward the mountains (on the nightly news you'll often hear "mauka showers", meaning showers near the mountains).
Mele Kalikimaka (may-lay ka-lee-kee-ma-ka) – Merry Christmas.
mu'u mu'u (moo-oo-moo-oo) – loose Hawaiian gown. Often pronounced as "moomoo".
na (na) – indicated plural when preceding a noun, thus *Na Mele O Maui* means *The Songs of Maui.*
'ohana (o-hah-na) – family, relatives.
'oi (oy) – best, as in *Maui no ka 'oi* ("Maui is the best").
'ono (oh-no) – delicious.
pali (pah-lee) – cliff, steep hill.
paniolo (pah-nee-oh-lo) – a Hawaiian cowboy.
pau (pow) – finished, completed, the end.
pilikia (pee-lee-kee-ah) – trouble of any kind.
po'okela (po-oh-kell-ah) – regarded the best by the community.
pono (poh-no) – richeous. An appropriate or balanced response.
pua (poo-uh) – flower.
puka (poo-kah) – hole, door, or entryway.
pupu (poo-poo) – appetizer, hors d'oeuvres.
tutu (too-too) – grandparent (not a Hawaiian word, but often used as slang/pidgin).
wahine (wa-hee-nay) – woman.
wai wai (why-why) – property or assets. Wai means water, and water is wealth in an agricultural community.
wikiwiki (wee-kee-wee-kee) – hurry.

BEST OF MAUI DINING

"Maui Onion" (oil on canvas) by Joan D. Arnold

When it comes to dining, the "Best of Maui" often means the "Best in the World." Maui is populated with many five star restaurants, including a few that just haven't been discovered yet by the critics. We profile a few of the Culinary Artists of Maui in the next few pages, followed by a detailed guide to the best Maui, and the world, has to offer.

VOTED BEST MAUI RESTAURANT

1996-Ilima Award
1997-Ilima Award
1998-Maui News

Bob Longhi is a man who loves to eat, and it shows in his restaurant with a vast menu that features the freshest ingredients available, cooked to perfection.

Bob Longhi not only created Maui's most popular restaurant, he also hosts the "Cooking with Longhi" TV show with sidekick Poppy Morgan. Learn to prepare seven of your favorite Longhi dishes at home with the new video "Cooking With Longhi". Gabrielle, Bob's daughter, has also illustrated four recipes in a beautiful portfolio suitable for framing. Bob says "anyone can be a great cook," and he proves it on his TV show and the video. Bob and Gabrielle also have a new book on food entitled "Longhi's" with recipes and reflections from Maui's most opinionated restaurateur. The video, portfolio and new book are all available at the restaurant.

Shrimp Longhi

Longhi's

A restaurant created by a man who loves to eat, Longhi's has been Maui's most successful restaurant for 20 years. It's easy to see why the Lahaina landmark, with spectacular ocean views, Casablanca decor with original island art, and consistently excellent food is a favorite of both resident and visitor.

The award winning menu ranges from huge 12oz. prime filets, giant Maine lobsters and sumptuous Pacific seafood to Longhi's famous pastas, fresh baked breads, and deserts. For the perfect wine, choose from their *Wine Spectator* award-winning wine list.

Mornings are a beautiful time to visit Lahaina, and Longhi's is open bright and early with home-baked cinnamon rolls, coffee cake, breakfast pastries, and buttermilk pancakes with real maple syrup. Also try their famous Italian frittatas and exotic melons flown in daily.

The Aloha spirit is alive at Longhi's, where the waiters and waitresses recite the menu. The food is always fresh and prepared in a style that is unique and original.

Eat when you are ready. Open from 7:30am to 10pm, serving breakfast, lunch and dinner, you never have to worry if you are too early or late. Come as you are, relax and enjoy a great meal in a casually elegant atmosphere among happy, friendly people. Reservations are accepted.

Longhi's, 888 Front Street, Lahaina; (808) 667-2288.

Prawns Amaretto, a Longhi's specialty.

Spectacular ocean views and decor are the perfect setting for the perfect meal.

MOUTH watering FOOD

ON THE WATERFRONT

The most ocean front restaurant on Maui!

Woody's serves up the freshest island fish, steaks grilled to perfection, and ono chicken and ribs daily. Enjoy creative cuisine from the best setting in Lahaina town.

Mouth watering food with breathtaking views . . .
the Hawaii you came here for!

WOODY'S ISLAND GRILL

839 Front Street, Lahaina, Maui • 661-8788 • From 11:00 AM
ON THE OCEAN INSIDE GARY'S ISLAND CLOTHING STORE

VOTED #1 JAPANESE RESTAURANT ON MAUI by Maui News Readers

KOBE
Japanese Steak House
and Oku's Sushi Bar

- Enjoy the exciting art of teppanyaki cooking. Knife-wielding chefs will prepare delicious steak, seafood, and chicken entrees right at your table.

- Super Sunset Specials available daily from 5:30 to 6:30pm.

- Join us for dancing and Karaoke with Toddy Lilikoi every Friday & Saturday from 9:30pm to closing.

Dinner nightly from 5:30-10pm.
Oku's fabulous Sushi until 11:30pm.
Reservations are recommended.

667-5555

136 Dickenson Street, Lahaina.
Free parking across the street
at the Baldwin House.

CHEESE 🌴 BURGER
· I · N · P·A·R·A·D·I·S·E· ®
Maui   Waikiki   Puerto Vallarta M.R.

WAIKIKI
2500 Kalakaua Ave.
(808) 923-3731

PUERTO VALLARTA
740 Paseo Diaz Ordaz

LAHAINA
811 Front Street
(808) 661-4855

BREAKFAST · LUNCH · DINNER

GUIDE TO TROPICAL DRINKS

SEX ON THE BEACH
Vodka, peach Schnapps, orange juice, cranberry juice. After one of these you can tell everyone you had "Sex on the Beach"!!

PIÑA COLADA
Light rum, pineapple juice, cream, coconut syrup.

LONG ISLAND ICE TEA
Vodka, gin, rum, tequila, and Triple Sec mixed with some sweet & sour and a splash of Coke™. Too many of these and you'll see whales even in the off season!

SUNSET PUNCH
Light, dark and 151 rum, pineapple and orange juice. Castaway's version of a Zombie.

What's a tropical island vacation without an exotic drink in hand to keep you cool and relaxed? Castaway's bartenders are experts at adding tropical twists to favorite island drinks. Add a sunset on the ocean and a refreshing island breeze, and you will seriously consider never leaving the islands. Castaway's Cafe received the Wine Spectator's Award for Excellence. You can find Kaanapali's best kept secret at the north end of Kaanapali in the Maui Kaanapali Villas and Resort.

MAI TAI
Start with light rum, add a little Orange Curacao, then orange and pineapple juices, a dash of grenadine, and a float of dark rum

BLUE HAWAII
A mixture of Vodka, pineapple juice, coconut syrup, Blue Curacao, and a dash of cream

LAVA FLOW
A blend of island rum, fresh bananas, cream, pineapple juice, coconut syrup and swirled with strawberries.

CASTAWAY'S SIGNATURE MANGO MADNESS
A great blend of light rum, mangoes, Sweet & Sour, Triple Sec, and lime juice.

CASTAWAY'S GREEN FLASH
Refreshing melon liquer, pineapple juice, fresh bananas, lime juice, and 151 rum. Be careful, you may see a green flash before the sun sets.

CHI CHI
A colada with a twist: Vodka, pineapple juice, cream, coconut syrup. Blend all ingredients with crushed ice and serve in a hurricane-style glass.

FRUIT DAIQUIRIS
Refreshing as the gentle tradewinds. Made with rum, Triple Sec, sweet & sour, and your choice of strawberry, banana, pineapple, mango, raspberry, or watermelon.

The Tropical Drinks recipes and photo are courtesy of:

Castaway Cafe is a full-service restaurant and bar, offering breakfast, lunch and dinner daily from 7:30am-9pm. Daily Happy Hour. Extensive wine list. Join us on Ka'anapali's North Beach in Maui Kaanapali Villas & Resort. See map on page 76. For more information call
661-9091

ISLAND FOODS

HAWAIIAN

poi — a starchy paste made from mashing cooked taro with a little bit of water; sometimes slightly fermented, poi is categorized as one, two or three finger poi by the thickness of its consistency.

kalua pig — a whole pig cooked in an imu, or underground oven.

laulau — pork, salted fish and taro leaves wrapped in ti or banana leaves and baked in an imu, steamed or broiled.

lomi salmon — lomi means massage, rub, press or squeeze in Hawaiian; the salmon usually raw, is worked with the fingers into a mixture of vinegar, onion and spices and eaten cold as a salad or side dish.

haupia — a pudding made of coconut crème.

'opihi — a limpet collected from shoreline rocks and considered a delicacy eaten raw or cooked.

'ulu — breadfruit, when cooked it tasted something like sweet potatoes.

hulihuli chicken — whole chickens roasted over a barbecue by turning (huli) rotisserie style.

poke — sliced raw fish or octopus mixed with salt, seaweed and chilipeppers.

KOREAN

kim chee — hot, spicy pickled cabbage and other vegetables.

kalbi — marinated, barbecued short ribs.

CHINESE

char siu — pork marinated in sugar, salt, soy sauce and red food coloring.

manapua – a dumpling the Chinese call dim sum, stuffed with meat and vegetables and baked, steamed or deep-fried.

JAPANESE

teriyaki — beef marinated in soy sauce.

tempura — vegetables or seafood deep-fried in batter.

shoyu — soy sauce.

sashimi — raw fish, usually ahi tuna, thinly sliced and served with green wasabe and soy sauce.

sushi — rice and bits of fish and vegetables wrapped in seaweed.

wasabi — spicy hot, green horseradish usually served with sushi and sashimi.

saimin — a popular noodle soup flavored with vegetables and beef.

bento — a take-out box lunch.

PORTUGUESE

malasada — donuts without holes.

bean soup — a rich spicy kidney bean soup with vegetables and Portuguese sausage.

GAME FISH

mahimahi — one of the least expensive and most common eating dish often referred to as dolphin but technically it is not; dolphins are mammals and mahimahi is a fish. Weighing 10 to 65 pounds, it has a broad head and body that tapers down to its tail; also known as Dorado.

a'u — the broad-billed swordfish or marlin, weighing up to 250 pounds each; not easy to catch, which is often reflected in its price, but excellent firm, moist, meaty steak like white flesh.

ono — also called wahoo or king mackerel, the name also means delicious in Hawaiian and certainly applies.

ulua — a prized, hard fighting game fish belonging to the "Jack Crevalle" family that ranges up to 125 pound; also known as pompano; sometimes caught by spear fisherman.

uku — the gray snapper.

ahi — yellowfin tuna, excellent cooked or raw and often found in sushi bars.

aku — bonito or skipjack tuna, a deep red-fleshed fish excellent cooked or raw as sashimi.

opakapaka — the pink snapper.

onaga — red snapper, a local favorite, caught in deep waters, with juicy, white tender meat.

One of Lahaina's Best Kept Secrets!

Enjoy fine romantic courtyard dining under the stars, surrounded by bougainvillea and serenaded with the sounds of Hawaiian music. Diners enjoy scrumptious island cuisine in generous portions.

Pioneer Inn Bar and Grill

Serving 6:30am until 10pm daily
Corner of Hotel and Wharf Streets

Phone: 808-661-3636
www.pioneerinnmaui.com

ISLAND DINING

A directory of the finest restaurants Maui has to offer.
*See the **Restaurant Dining Chart** on page 40 for more information.*

ALOHA MIXED PLATE
1285 Front Street, Lahaina
(808) 661-3322
Visit Aloha Mixed Plate for "ono" Hawaiian-style, Hawaiian-sized meals. Enjoy outdoor dining at the water's edge at this charming eatery located just oceanside of the Lahaina Cannery Mall. Voted "Best Plate Lunch" on the island two years running by The Maui News readers in the newspaper's annual restaurant poll, the extensive menu features Maui's best local-style plate lunches, juicy hamburgers, delicious mahimahi burgers, shoyu chicken, chili and rice, and a variety of fresh noodle dishes. Hawaiian Plate, Daily Specials and Happy Hour Specials every single day! Aloha Mixed Plate is open daily from 10:30 a.m. - 10:00 p.m. Take-out orders available. Map page 68, ad page 34.

B.J.'S CHICAGO PIZZERIA
730 Front Street, Lahaina
(808) 661-0700
Cool Pacific breezes bathe you as you dine at this upstairs Front Street eatery. Enjoy one of the best ocean, harbor, and sunset views on the island. At night, the open-air dining room is filled with beautiful Hawaiian melodies blending with the rhythmic sea, live on the "Ocean Front Stage." Judged as having one of the "Mainland's" Best Pizzas by Bon Apetit Magazine, L.A. Times, and Orange County Register, along with a Best Pizza award by Maui News, BJ's has quickly become one of Maui's "Must Dos." Old plantation decor and historic photos complement home recipe pizza, pastas, salads, and sandwiches that have won raves from all over the island. Great food, magical atmosphere, and unbelievable sunsets. No wonder BJ's is considered among the islands best values. Map page 69; ad page 33.

CASTAWAY BEACH CAFE
Maui Kaanapali Villas & Resort, Kaanapali
(808) 661-9091
Come join us oceanside on Kaanapali Beach at our popular local cafe and watering hole. We are a full-service restaurant offering breakfast, lunch and dinner. Our hours are 7:30am-9pm. The beauty of this island oasis is the view, but the food's great, too! Some specialties for breakfast include macadamia nut pancakes, eggs benedict, and Kula cinnamon french toast. For lunch try our great paradise chicken salad or one of our specialty burgers. We have all the island favorites for dinner including fresh fish and our famous coconut shrimp. So if you're in the mood for a casual dining experience or a great sunset happy hour, Castaway Cafe is your place! Come see our friendly crew for great food, affordable prices, and lots of Aloha. Wine Spectator Award for Excellence. Map page 76, ad page 30.

CHEESEBURGER IN PARADISE
811 Front St., Lahaina • (808) 661-4855
2500 Kalakaua Ave.,Waikiki • (808) 923-3731
740 Paseo Diaz Ordaz, Puerto Vallarta
This is one of those places you'd hoped to find on your vacation to paradise... great food, fun atmosphere, authentic Hawaiian decor, and awesome location! The legendary Cheeseburger in Paradise/Maui has two floors of spectacular harbor and ocean views. Every seat is a good one! Same goes for their Waikiki eatery that sports magnificent views of the classic surf breaks where Duke Kahanamoku became a legend, and don't forget to check out their newest location in Puerto Vallarta, on your next trip to Mexico; dining on the Malecon, right on the Bay of Banderas. Selections range from salads and chicken dishes to their world famous "Cheeseburger In Paradise." Cheeseburgers, Mai-Tais and Rock 'n'

Roll is the theme with live tropical entertainment nightly from sunset 'til closing. The family will rave about this experience when they get back home. The restaurants and retail stores are open daily for breakfast, lunch and dinner. Although no reservations are taken, the wait, when there is one, is usually no longer than 10 to 15 minutes and is definitely worth it! Map page 68, ad page 29.

CHINA BOAT RESTAURANT
4474 L. Honoapiilani Hwy., Kahana
(808) 669-5089
Come in and experience the finest Chinese Cuisine at the China Boat Restaurant, a local as well as a visitor favorite for years. Nominated best restaurant for the category of Chinese Cuisine by the Maui News, 1997 and 1999. The atmosphere is authentic. Their food is prepared fresh daily. They also offer seafood specialties and special family dinners for 2 or more. The China Boat Restaurant is located just 7 miles north of Lahaina. Turn left at the Kahana Gateway Shopping Center then right on the lower road for about a 1/4 mile it is on your right. When you arrive you will be greeted by a friendly and courteous family-owned restaurant. The China Boat Restaurant is open for lunch or dinner. Call for reservations at 669-5089. Take-out is available. Delivery from Kaanapali to Kapalua. Map page 81, ad page 33.

THE COFFEE STORE
Napili Plaza • (808) 669-4170
Kaahumanu Center • (808) 871-6860
Maalaea Triangle • (808) 242-2779
Azeka Place, Kihei • (808) 875-4244
Voted "Best Coffee Shop on Maui" for 6 years by the Maui News Reader's Poll. While visiting the beautiful Island of Maui, make sure you save time to relax with a delicious drink at The Coffee Store. You won't believe how much more flavor and aroma our

freshly roasted coffee has until you try it yourself! We use the finest quality beans, roast them in small batches daily right here in our stores and brew them to perfection. Our stores also feature gourmet deli-style meals prepared on-the-spot and a large selection of tantalizing pastries and desserts. If you aren't a coffee drinker, we also have a variety of delicious teas, whole fruit smoothies and many unique gifts. You can even enjoy the "Taste of Aloha" after you fly home by having us ship freshly roasted coffee beans right to your doorstep. Visit our web site at www.mauicoffee.com or call us toll free at 1-800-327-9661. Once you try our famous Kona coffee, you will be "hooked for life"! Aloha... Map page 14, 81, 94, ad page 79.

COMPADRES BAR & GRILL

Lahaina Cannery Mall, facing the ocean
1221 Honoapiilani Hwy, Lahaina
(808) 661-7189

Award-winning Compadres acclaimed for its creative Mexican cuisine with California/Arizona accents, offers traditional favorites, fresh-island fish, grilled specialties and such unique dishes as Maui-style Potato Chip Nachos. Enjoy breakfast, lunch and dinner, complete with a full selection of imported Mexican beers and the best margaritas on Maui! Breakfast from 8am, lunch and dinner from 11am. Map page 68, ad page 39.

EDO JAPAN RESTAURANT

Lahaina Cannery Mall • (808) 661-7784
Kaahumanu Center, Kahului • 877-7784

Quick service teppanyaki-style restaurant. Try the delicious yakisoba dishes: Grilled noodles served over fresh steamed vegetables and topped with your choice of grilled meat with mushrooms. Also serving sushi, noodles and rice bowls with special toppings. Open daily from 10:30am to 9pm. No reservations needed. Map page 68 & 14, ad page 45.

HECOCKS

505 Front Street, Lahaina
(808) 661-8810

South Lahaina's "best kept secret"! Located at 505 Front Street on the ocean (makai) side, with magnificent

BJ's Chicago Pizzeria

Live Contemporary Island Music Nightly
Featuring Hawaii's Top Recording Artists

"One of the Countries Best"-Bon Apetite

"Top Five Pizzas"-L.A. Times

"Voted Best Pizza on Maui"
-Maui News Reader's Poll

"Maui's Best Pizza!"-Paradise Family Guide

Appetizers • Homebaked Sandwiches • Salads • Pizza • Desserts • Unique Tropical Drinks

730 Front St., Lahaina, At the Seawall, 11am-11pm
(808) 661-0700

CHINA BOAT
Maui's Finest Chinese Cuisine

Prepared fresh daily • Authentic atmosphere
Lunch 11:30am-2pm • Dinner 5pm-10pm
Delivery from Kaanapali to Kapalua
Take Out Available

4474 L. Honoapiilani Rd, Kahana • 669-5089
7 miles north of Lahaina

HECOCKS
Oceanfront Dining
Cocktails
LAHAINA, MAUI

"South Lahaina's Best Kept Secret!"

Oceanfront dining with three-island view and beautiful sunsets

661-8810

Italian/American Restaurant & Cocktail Lounge on the Ocean at 505 Front Street in Lahaina.

email: hecocks@aol.com

ALOHA MIXED PLATE

"BEST PLATE LUNCH"
—MAUI NEWS READERS POLL

"BEST PUPU – COCONUT PRAWNS"
—1999 TASTE OF LAHAINA

Join us on our deck for beachside plate lunches, burgers, noodles and "ono" daily specials. Casual, affordable and fun!

1285 Front Street - Makai (Oceanside) of Lahaina Cannery Mall

661-3322

Call us about our "Aloha Friday" Specials

ISLAND DINING

oceanfront views and sunsets of three Hawaiian Islands. Delicious Italian/ American cuisine made from Grandma Lapadura's fine Italian family recipes. Also enjoy an Aloha cocktail at the oceanview lounge. Open for breakfast, lunch and dinner with daily specials. For reservations, call us at 661-8810. Also email us at hecocks@aol.com. Map page 69, ad page 34.

KIHEI KALAMA VILLAGE
1941 S. Kihei Road, Kihei
Across from Kalama Park
(808) 879-6610
A favorite destination for local residents and visitors. This inviting Hawaiian plantation setting is a one-stop eclectic mix of shops and theme restaurants for the whole family to enjoy. Over 40 shops feature an unusual and appealing selection of gifts, crafts and souvenirs. A variety of 10 restaurants serves breakfast, lunch, dinner and tropical drinks daily at reasonable prices. Menus items include Mexican, Greek, Thai, local entrees, fresh fish, salads, sandwiches and burgers. Ample free parking. Map page 94; ad page 97.

KOBE JAPANESE STEAK HOUSE AND OKU'S SUSHI BAR
136 Dickenson Street, Lahaina
(808) 667-5555
Enjoy the exciting, ancient art of teppanyaki cooking at the restaurant voted #1 Japanese Restaurant on Maui. Knife-wielding chefs will prepare delicious steak, seafood, and chicken entrees right at your table. Oku's fabulous sushi will complete your Japanese dining experience. Dinner nightly from 5:30 to 10:00pm with Super Sunset Specials available for the first hour. Oku's Sushi Bar is open nightly until 11:30pm. Join us for dancing and Karaoke every Friday and Saturday from 9:30pm to closing. Reservations are recommended. Call 667-5555. Free parking across the street at the Baldwin House. All major credit cards accepted. Map page 69, ad page 28.

ISLAND DINING

LONGHI'S
888 Front Street, Lahaina
(808) 667-2288
Coming soon to The Shops at Wailea
Longhi's is Maui's most successful and popular restaurant. Black and white tiled decor sets the stage for a colorful selection of Italian cuisine featuring only the freshest ingredients. The waiters and waitresses recite the fresh, original changing fare of seafood, pastas, homemade breads, prime steaks, chicken, veal, and fresh vegetables. And don't forget the perfect additions to your meals, including a Wine Spectator award-winning wine list and a dessert tray to die for! Serving breakfast, lunch and dinner. Open daily 7:30am-10pm. Reservations suggested. Map page 68 & 94; ad page 26.

MAUI COFFEE COMPANY
123 Bay Drive • The Kapalua Shops
(808) 669-9667
Maui Coffee Company is a beautiful espresso and lunch bar located in the tropical courtyard of The Kapalua Shops next to the Kapalua Bay Hotel. Relax with a cappuccino made from the finest fresh roasted Kona coffees available. Casual lunches and snacks compliment our famous island fresh fruit smoothies. A short walk from the Kapalua beach and you could be enjoying a creamy frozen mocha. Yum! Open seven days a week, 9am-6pm. Map page 81.

MAUI COFFEE ROASTERS
444 Hana Hwy., Kahului
(808) 877-2877 • Fax: (808) 871-2684
Toll free: 1-800-645-2877
website: www.hawaiiancoffee.com
Why is Maui Coffee Roasters so popular? It's because this family-owned business roasts and brews some of the best coffee on Maui. Add the best coffee prices on the island and you start to see why residents and visitors alike flock to this unique caffeine oasis. Kona, along with selected coffees from Maui, Kauai and Molokai, are fresh roasted daily. They also have a savory food selection. It ranges from the ulti-

Now at Honolulu's Restaurant Row, too!

If you love it raw, wait 'til you taste it cooked!

Top Food Rating – Zagat Survey

Acclaimed in *Wine Spectator*

Honolulu Magazine Hale 'Aina Multiple Award Winner

Sansei
Seafood Restaurant & Sushi Bar

"Best of Maui" Multiple Award Winner

"A Taste of Lahaina" Multiple Award Winner

"Ulupalakua Thing" Multiple Award Winner

115 Bay Drive (The Shops at Kapalua), Kapalua , Maui • (808) 669-OCTO (6286)

THE FEAST AT LELE

"This is the most fabulous cooking on Maui, which is saying a lot."
—*Travel & Leisure*

"an intimate experience with 'upto date' Polynesian cuisine.. the entertainment is top-notch."
—*Travel Holiday*

Journey through the islands of Polynesia in a celebration of cuisine, dance and song. Along the beach in historic Lahaina town.

Brought to you by the creators of Old Lāhaina Lū'au & Pacific'O Restaurant

Reservations are recommended:

667-LELE (5353)
505 Front Street, Lahaina

mate veggie burger to lunch specials of Hawaiian lobster and fresh Hawaiian fish. Whether you're on the isle of Maui or at home, Maui Coffee Roasters will ship to you. Ordering couldn't be simpler... use their toll-free number, fax, email, or order from their website at www.hawaiiancoffee.com. Map page 14. Ad page 49.

MAUI MARRIOTT LUAU
Maui Marriott Hotel,
Kaanapali Beach
(808) 661-LUAU (661-5828)
The Marriott Luau is renowned for its sumptuous feast and spectacular entertainment on breathtaking Kaanapali Beach. Each guest is greeted and adorned with a traditional shell lei. After a demonstration of island games and cultural activities, the imu ceremony begins. A kalua pig is dug out and prepared in the underground oven where it has spent hours roasting to

perfection. The buffet showcases chicken Polynesian, broiled teriyaki beef steak, Island fish, lomi lomi salmon, fresh salads, poi (of course), unique desserts, and much more. Don't forget an exotic mai tai from the open bar. Dinner is followed by a Polynesian odyssey of song, dance and historic chants performed by a troupe of brightly-costumed entertainers. The evening reaches its peak with the spectacular Triple Fireknife performance. No visit to the Hawaiian Islands is complete without the experience of an authentic luau, and the Marriott Luau is one that you'll savor and remember for a long time afterward. Map on page 76, ad page 77.

MAUI MARRIOTT RESTAURANTS
100 Nohea Kai Drive, Kaanapali
(808) 667-1200, Ext. 51
"Eat healthy and enjoy your dining experience" has always been the motto

of the Maui Marriott Resort & Ocean Club, according to Executive Chef Brendan Mahoney. With the redesign and addition of exciting new restaurants, this motto still holds true. You'll also find that some things never change, such as the superb quality of food, friendly service and enchanting atmosphere. Stunning sunset views are an added bonus. Opening August 2000, Va Bene, the resort's new main dining room, will tempt guests with flavorful Italian cuisine, complete with an antipasti bar, a breakfast buffet and a walk-up bar. This beachfront bistro, formerly the Nikko Restaurant, offers magnificent ocean views and indoor-outdoor oceanfront seating. The famous Makai Bar will be transformed by December 2000 into the Nalu Sunset Bar & Sushi, a full-service bar with a Hawaiian-style sushi counter. An all-new deck area provides guests with front-seat viewing of the ocean

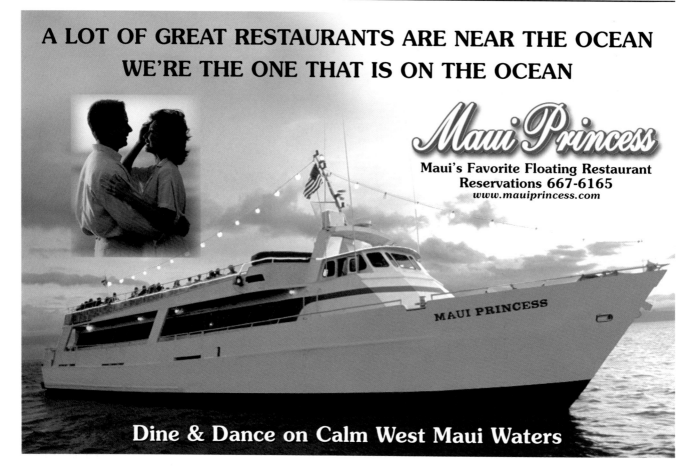

ISLAND DINING

while enjoying tropical cocktails. December 2000, the Kau Kau Grill & Bar will become the new Beach Walk Market & Pantry. Take a walk along this marketplace and delight in everything you could want in a corner store, from hot entrees and salads to deli cuisine and ice cream. Guests may also take a break with breakfast and lunch and dine on hot grill items, salads, sandwiches, fruits and juices. Don't forget a truly Hawaiian experience at the oceanfront Marriott Luau, featured nightly from 5-8 p.m. The show includes complimentary leis, Hawaiian crafts and games, an imu/roast pig ceremony, open bar reception, an exciting Polynesian dance revue, lavish buffet dinner and Mai Tai cocktails. For more information and renovation updates, please call guest services at (808) 667-1200. Please note that due to renovations, restaurant and luau operations, dates and times may vary. Please call for reservations and current information. Map page 76.

MAUI PRINCESS
DINNER CRUISE
Slip #3 Lahaina Harbor
(808) 667-6165
www.mauiprincess.com

Enjoy an evening of dining and dancing on Maui's largest charter yacht. Dine on the large open air upper deck of this spacious 120' stabilized ship. Take in spectacular sunset views while dining on Filet Mignon AND half a chicken, fresh salad with papaya seed dressing, baked potato, vegetable du jour and dessert. Vegetarian options available. Enjoy the full open bar. After dinner, dance on the large dance floor to live music. Sailing on calm West Maui waters every evening. Map page 69; ad page 36.

FOR MORE INFORMATION SEE OUR HANDY DINING CHART ON PAGE 40.

OLD LĀHAINA LŪ'AU
Traditional Hula and Feast

Frommer's '99 Maui —
"Its authenticity, intimacy, hospitality, cultural integrity and sheer romantic beauty have made this Maui's top luau"

Hawaii Magazine —
"This is the best luau on Maui. I rate it the best in the state."

Featured in National Geographic Traveler Magazine

OLD LĀHAINA LŪ'AU

Join Us for Maui's Best Luau
Front Street, Lahaina...
Oceanside of Lahaina Cannery Mall

For Reserved Seats Call
661-9021

www.OldLahainaLuau.com

ISLAND DINING

MAUI TACOS

5095 Napilihau St, Napili Plaza • 665-0222
Lahaina Square, Lahaina • 661-8883
Kamaole Beach Center, Kihei • 879-5005
Ka'ahumanu Center Food Court, Kahului
Prince Kuhio Plaza, Hilo
Georgia, Florida, New York, Delaware
www.mauitacos.com

Absolutely the best Mexican food in Hawaii! All the basic recipes are authentic - they come from the grandmother of the Executive Chef. Former chef/owner of Avalon, Mark Ellman, insists on flavor and quality using only the freshest ingredients. Maui Tacos features grilled steak, chicken and island fresh fish served in tacos, burritos, etc. Maui Tacos also offers at each location a "Free Salsa Bar" featuring five salsas. All menu items are made to order using the best and freshest ingredients available, something for which Ellman is well known. Maui Tacos is now franchising on the Mainland, for information visit their website at www.mauitaco.com or call 888-628-4822. Map page 14, 68, 81, and 94, ad page 79.

PIONEER INN RESTAURANT

Best Western Pioneer Inn
Corner of Front Street/Banyan Tree and Hotel Street, Lahaina.
(808) 661-3636

Located on Front Street across from the famous Banyan Tree on the Lahaina Harbor and the site of the first lighthouse in the Pacific is the Historic Pioneer Inn. The Pioneer Inn, Hawaii's second oldest hotel, is registered by the Historic American Building Survey and recorded in the archives of the Library of Congress. The Pioneer Inn features the Best Western Pioneer Inn Hotel, 18 Shops and Merchants, the world-renowned Whalers Saloon, the Banyan Tree Cafe, and Snug Harbor Restaurant. The Banyan Tree Cafe and Whalers Saloon Restaurant serves both breakfast, lunch, pupus, and cocktails from 6:30am. Snug Harbor is open for dinner from 5:30pm with your choice of service in the lush tropical

Courtyard, on the Sunset Lanai, or in the Dining Room. Snug Harbor is also available for weddings, private parties and conferences. The Pioneer Inn Restaurants feature a mix of American and Hawaiian Cuisines utilizing fresh fish including the catch of the day by local fishermen off the Wharf, and local ingredients. Whether it's an oceanscape, the tropical breeze, or the ambiance of the 97-year-old Pioneer Inn, you will be reminded of the special beauty and rich history of Hawaii when dining at the Pioneer Inn. The warm and hospitable staff at the Pioneer Inn welcomes all to the heart of Lahaina. Map page 69; ad page 31.

PIZZA PARADISO—ITALIAN CAFFÉ

Honokowai Marketplace
(808) 667-2929 • FREE DELIVERY

Pizza Paradiso is an Italian Caffé offering inexpensive gourmet cuisine in a casual setting. Voted "Best Pizza on Maui" two years in a row by a *Maui News Reader's Poll*, Pizza Paradiso serves an all-day menu of gourmet pizza (whole or by the slice), a large selection of pasta dishes, gourmet panini (sandwiches) crostini and salads. On the sweet side there's smoothies, ice cream, sundaes, and assorted cakes. Their homemade tiramisu has been named "The Best Dessert on Maui." Open 11am-10pm serving lunch and dinner, with free delivery available. Map page 76, ad page 39.

PIZZA PARADISO

Whalers Village, Kaanapali
(808) 667-0333 • FREE DELIVERY

The original Pizza Paradiso located right off the beach in Kaanapali offers the same gourmet pizza as their Honokowai location. Voted "Best Pizza on Maui" 1998 and 1999 by a *Maui News Reader's Poll*. This smaller location offers some of the pasta selections as well as salads, crostini and sandwiches. Open 11am-10pm serving lunch and dinner. Map page 76, ad page 39.

SANSEI SEAFOOD RESTAURANT AND SUSHI BAR

The Shops at Kapalua
115 Bay Drive, Kapalua
(808) 669-OCTO (669-6286)

In a few short years, this small, out-of-the-way restaurant has received accolades usually reserved for those which have risen to national and international acclaim. The most prestigious honor came in the 1998 Zagat Hawai'i Restaurant Survey, considered by many to be the "Foodie Bible," in which Sansei received the highest rating for food in the State of Hawai'i. And it held onto its first place status in the 1999 Survey as well. The restaurant has also won Hawai'i's most distinguished culinary honor, the Honolulu magazine Hale 'Aina award, as one of Maui's best restaurants for two consecutive years. And it's won numerous "Best of Maui" honors in annual Maui News readers' polls and "A Taste of Lahaina" prizes for such innovative signature dishes as Asian Rock Shrimp Cake and Crab & Mango Mamenori Handroll. The force behind the food is Executive Chef/Owner Dave "D.K." Kodama. This O'ahu native with many years of international culinary experience has combined his own Japanese heritage with Hawai'i's incredible ethnic mix and the flavors he experienced in his travels to create a style very much his own. The fabulous Sansei dining adventure begins upon opening the menus. The sushi menu is so creative and big and tantalizing diners find they must return again and again to try it all. The anything-but-regular dinner menu features items like Nori Ravioli of Shrimp and Salmon with Shiitake Mushroom Sauce, Macadamia Nut Crusted Australian Rack of Lamb with Gorgonzola and Garlic Smashed Potatoes and Sweet Miso Sauce, and on and on, each item more mouth-watering than the one before. There's a whole slew of specials offered every evening and for those who think unkindly on dessert at sushi restaurants, minds are changed here.

ISLAND DINING

Dinner is served nightly from 5:30pm; karaoke on Thursdays & Fridays from 10:00pm to closing. Map page 81; ad page 35.

WOODY'S OCEANFRONT GRILL
839 Front Street, Lahaina
(808) 661-8788
Woody's offers the best oceanfront views in Lahaina from two dining levels. Street-level guests can almost touch the blue Pacific as it laps gently against the building's pilings. The views from both street-level and the upstairs tables and bar area are truly the best in town, encompassing Lahaina Harbor and the neighboring islands of Moloka'i and Lana'i. Sunsets year 'round are breathtaking. Woody's features a delicious, delightful, and affordable menu with items to please every palate, including island style burgers and ribs, and the freshest of salads. Just a few of the dishes already receiving rave reviews from diners are: Portobello Mushroom Fritters, Grilled Miso Prawns with Mango Sauce, Woody's Island Ribs, and the freshest catch of the day. Located within Gary's Island retail store, the restaurant is bright and airy, with decor reminiscent of a 1940s local beach home. Diners are encouraged to explore the fantastic collection of period Hawaiiana displayed throughout the restaurant. Lunch and dinner are served at Woody's from 11am to 10pm daily; the bar is open until 11pm with pupus served at the bar until closing. Map page 68, ad page 27.

FOR MORE INFORMATION SEE OUR HANDY DINING CHART ON THE NEXT PAGE

COMPADRES
BAR & GRILL

FESTIVE MEXICAN DINING AND A GREAT PLACE TO PARTY!

Voted "Favorite Mexican Restaurant" by Honolulu Magazine readers, Compadres features "Western Cooking with a Mexican Accent"

LAHAINA CANNERY MALL, LAHAINA (808) 661-7189

PIZZA PARADISO
Italian Caffé

Don't miss our award-winning pastas & tiramisu

"The best pizza I ever had"
—*Frommer's Guide*

Voted "Best Pizza on Maui"
—*Maui News Reader's Poll 1998, 99*

Try our delicious salads and gourmet sandwiches

Lunch and Dinner • Dine In or Take Out

Free Delivery

Honokowai Marketplace
667-2929

Whalers Village Food Court
667-0333

BEST OF MAUI DINING GUIDE

Your quick and easy reference guide to the Best restaurants Maui has to offer. Also see the directory listings beginning on page 32. Please note this information is subject to change.

CREDIT CARD KEY: V=Visa; MC=MasterCard; DC=Diner's Club; JCB=Japanese Credit Bureau; AE=American Express; DISC=Discover	BREAKFAST/ LUNCH/ DINNER	CREDIT CARDS	ENTER-TAINMENT	FULL SERVICE BAR	PAGE
ALOHA MIXED PLATE 1285 Front Street, Lahaina • (808) 661-3322	L/D	V/MC/AE	•	•	34
B.J.'S CHICAGO PIZZERIA 730 Front Street, Lahaina • (808) 661-0700	L/D	V/MC/DC/AE	•	•	33
CASTAWAY BEACH CAFE Maui Kaanapali Villas & Resort, Kaanapali • (808) 661-9091	B/L/D	DC/DISC/AE/V/MC	•	•	30
CHEESEBURGER IN PARADISE 811 Front St., Lahaina • (808) 661-4855	B/L/D	V/MC/AE/DISC/JCB	•	•	29
CHINA BOAT RESTAURANT 4474 L. Honoapiilani Hwy., Kahana • (808) 669-5089	L/D	V/MC/AE		•	33
THE COFFEE STORE Napili Plaza, Napili • (808) 669-4170	B/L/D	V/MC/AX			79
COMPADRES BAR & GRILL Lahaina Cannery Mall, Lahaina • (808) 661-7189	B/L/D	V/MC/DC/AX/DISC		•	39
EDO JAPAN Lahaina Cannery Mall, Lahaina • (808) 661-7784	L/D	CASH ONLY			45
HECOCKS 505 Front Street, Lahaina • (808) 661-8810	B/L/D	V/MC/DC		•	34
KOBE JAPANESE STEAKHOUSE 136 Dickenson St., Lahaina • (808) 667-5555	D	ALL MAJOR	•	•	28
LONGHI'S 888 Front Street, Lahaina • (808) 667-2288	B/L/D	V/MC/AE/DISC	•	•	26
MAUI COFFEE ROASTERS 444 Hana Highway, Kahului • (808) 877-CUPS	Cafe/Latte	V/MC/AE			49
MAUI PRINCESS DINNER CRUISE Slip #3 Lahaina Harbor (808) 667-6165 • www.mauiprincess.com	B/L/D	V/MC/AE	•	•	36
MAUI TACOS Napili Plaza, 5095 Napilihau St, Napili • (808) 665-0222 Lahaina Square, Lahaina • 661-8883 Kamaole Beach Center, Kihei • 879-5005 Ka'ahumanu Center Food Court, Kahului	B/L/D	CASH ONLY			79
PIONEER INN RESTAURANT Corner of Front Street/Banyan Tree and Hotel Street, Lahaina. • (808) 661-3636	B/L/D	V/MC/AE/DC/JCB	•	•	31
PIZZA PARADISO—ITALIAN CAFFÉ Honokowai Marketplace, Honokowai • (808) 667-2929	B/L/D	V/MC		BEER/WINE	39
PIZZA PARADISO—FOOD COURT Whalers Village, Kaanapali • (808) 667-0333	L/D	CASH ONLY			39
SANSEI SEAFOOD RESTAURANT AND SUSHI BAR The Shops at Kapalua 115 Bay Drive, Kapalua • (808) 669-6286	D	V/MC/AE/JCB/DC	•	•	35
WOODY'S OCEANFRONT GRILL 839 Front Street, Lahaina • (808) 661-8788	L/D	V/MC/AE	•	•	27

BEST OF MAUI SHOPPING

"Aumakua with Kukui" (oil on canvas) by Joan D. Arnold

The selection of shops on Maui is as diverse as the people of Maui. From aloha clothing to art galleries featuring world famous local artists, rare precious jewelry to rare tropical birds, you'll find it all right here in paradise.

SHOPS & GALLERIES

A directory of the unique shops and world-class galleries Maui has to offer.

C. ARNOLD BUILDING DESIGNS
P.O. Box 10669, Lahaina
(808) 669-4439 • Fax: (808) 669-0037
Email: homeplan4u@aol.com

C. Arnold Building Designs provides Architectural Drafting for homes, additions, condominium remodels, decks, restaurant layout, drawings for committee decisions and commercial space. They meet on-site to discuss layout and design to use the full potential of your property. If you are looking for affordable building plans please call (808) 669-4439. Ad page 48.

CARLSON-WAGONLIT TRAVEL
KLAHANI TRAVEL
Lahaina Cannery Mall
1221 Honoapiilani Hwy, Lahaina
(808) 667-2712 • Fax (808) 661-5875
Toll free: 1-800-669-MAUI (6284)
Email: klahanitvl@aol.com
Website: www.klahani.com

Lahaina's full-service travel agency located at the Lahaina Cannery Mall, home of Safeway and Long's Drugs. Lots of free parking and convenient to everyone. Mainland air, low-priced inter-island travel, air/room/car packages, hotels and condos. Hawaii's Cruise Store — all destinations, all lines. Map page 68. Ad page 44.

CHANEL BOUTIQUE
2435 Kaanapali Pkwy (Whalers Village)
Lahaina, HI 96761 • (808) 661-1555

To walk into the CHANEL Boutique in Maui is to walk into the heart of Paris. Designed in the spirit of the original CHANEL Boutique in Paris, the Boutique opened its doors in May 1995, as the third CHANEL Boutique in the islands of Hawaii. Just steps from the beach, you'll find Ready-to-Wear designed by Karl Lagerfeld, world-renowned CHANEL fragrances, fashion accessories, LE TEMPS CHANEL watch collection, jewelry and a full line of cosmetics and treatment. Superbly-trained consultants give you the latest information on makeup and skincare to make you feel like a million dollars. Classic decor elements of Mademoiselle CHANEL's renowned style accent the interior including: black lacquer cabinets, beige suede sofas, marble floors and a dazzling reflection of mirrors. In Maui, Open 7 days a week from 10:00am to 10:00pm. Map page 76; ad on back cover.

COLLECTORS FINE ART OF HAWAII
Hyatt Regency Maui • (808) 661-1032
201 Nohea Kai Drive, Suite 21
Lahaina, HI 96761

The most exciting and eclectic gallery on Maui is the beautiful Collectors Fine Art. The dedicated artists represented in this unique gallery are special people whose art brings joy, healing, understanding and an expression of freedom to our lives. The diverse selection of art invites the viewer to explore, through an artist's vision, the world of color and excitement. Hawaii's Premier Gallery, Collectors Fine Art offers its numerous private, and corporate collectors around the world only the finest in quality art at affordable prices. The gallery is equally dedicated to those who may know little of the workings of art, but yet, are intuitively moved by the presence of new creative expression. Highlights of the gallery include the works of a number of internationally known artists including several who reside and create their art in the islands. Collectors Fine Art also offers a broad selection of related services, including appraisals, collection consultations, local delivery, on-site exhibition of artworks, and professional interior design assistance. The friendly, knowledgeable staff at Collectors Fine Art invite you to visit this beautiful gallery where there are frequent mini-concerts and complimentary wine in the evening. Located in the prestigious Hyatt Regency Hotel, Kaanapali. Collectors Fine Art is open daily from 9am to 10pm. Map page 76; ad page 3.

DAN'S GREENHOUSE
133 Prison St., Lahaina
(808) 661-8412

Maui's most exotic shop, Dan's Greenhouse offers hand-fed baby birds, monkeys, certified pot belly pigs, tropical and exotic plants, all available for export or by mail order. And if you're looking for a Fuku Bonsai tree like you see at all the restaurants around the island, Dan's is the exclusive dealer. Dan's has baby parrots of all sizes that are tame and very friendly, including a rare Black Palm Cockatoo worth $25,000 and available for adoption. An exotic experience awaits you at Dan's Greenhouse. Map page 69; ad page 47.

DFS GALLERIA HAWAII
Island Essentials Maui
Whalers Village, Kaanapali
(808) 667-5111
Website: www.dfsgalleria.com

You're in for a pleasant surprise when you visit DFS Galleria at Whalers Village. Whether you're an international or domestic traveler or local resident, you will discover a store full of island surprises for yourself or that special someone. DFS Galleria Maui features the finest duty-free merchandise for international travelers. Discover a wide assortment of brand names such as Salvatore Ferragamo, Fendi, Burberry, Cartier and more. Shop for men's and women's leathergoods, fine watches, jewelry, fashion apparel and accessories, all at duty-free prices. DFS Galleria Maui also features a large assortment of merchandise available for general purchase including sunglasses, watches, leathergoods, surfwear and fashion apparel from the most popular brands. Visit Island Essential Maui — a cosmetic, fragrance and body care specialty store located on the main level of Whalers Village. You'll find a full line of cosmetics and fragrances from Calvin Klein, Chanel, Christian Dior, Estee Lauder, Clinique, Lancome, MAC, Hard Candy, and much more. All merchandise at Island Essentials Maui is available for general purchase. We welcome you to the beautiful island of Maui and invite you to discover DFS Galleria and Island Essentials Maui. Map page 76. Ad page 55.

GARYS ISLAND
839 Front Street, Lahaina
(808) 662-0424

Garys Island Dick's Last Resort is a vibrant and exciting fashion creation featuring complete resort wear from head to toe for men, women and kids. Garys Island carries many well known brands such as Reyn Spooner, Tori Richard, Kahala, Back East, Tommy Bahama and many more. In addition to specializing in the "Aloha Shirt," Garys Island displays an array of different styles such as motif prints and artist collections in shirts, shorts, pants, dresses and skirts. To complete your island attire select from a unique assortment of accessories including hats, resort bags, towels, sunglasses and jewelry; as well as the finest resort footwear found anywhere. We at Garys Island pride ourselves on creating a store with a unique and exciting atmosphere that provides outstanding customer service. It

ANDREA SMITH
Images of the Eternal Expression of the Spirit

"A Beautiful Day" by Andrea Smith
Original mixed media on paper 30" x 44";
limited edition on canvas: 18" x 24" and 30" x 40" (#4298)

"Lei Maker" by Andrea Smith
Original mixed media on paper 30" x 22";
limited edition on canvas: 18" x 24", 20" x 30", 30" x 40" (#4295)

MATTHEW SMITH
Experience the Journey through multicolor works rich in Symbolism and Color

"Memories of the Night" by Matthew Smith
Original oil & acrylic on paper 22" x 10"

Lahaina Gallery • 728 Front St., Lahaina • 808/667-2152
Kapalua Gallery • 123 Bay Dr., The Kapalua Shops • 808/669-0202
Lahaina Gallery • The Shops at Wailea

Andrea Smith Fine Art • Lahaina, Hawaii • 1-800-369-1205
Web page: http://www.andreasmith.com • email: asfaltd@aol.com

LAHAINA CANNERY MALL

LAHAINA MOTORCYCLE WORKS

Harley-Davidson™ Tee-Shirts, Watches, Aloha Wear, Gifts, Collectibles and Jewelry.
661-6603

Carlson Wagonlit Travel®

KLAHANI TRAVEL

A Full Service travel agency. Overnighters to all islands. Low-Priced Interisland Air. Condos, Hotels, Cars: Hawaii & Worldwide. Vacation Rentals on Maui. Cruise Ships: All Desinations, All Cruise Lines (featuring Royal Caribbean, Princess, Crystal, Radisson & Seaborn). 667-2712; Mainland Toll Free: 1-800-669-MAUI (6284)

MAUI TREASURES

Maui Treasures carries quality arts and sculptures, collection jewelry, Hawaiian products, t-shirts and more at affordable prices. It's your one-stop shop to find the most unique gifts to take home from Maui.
661-1131

Discover the Difference!

ROLAND'S SHOES

Give your feet a vacation. Men, Women and Children's name brand shoes and sandals, plus handbags and accessories. Also located at Maui Mall (in Kahului) and Azeka Place II (in Kihei). **661-8114**

TOTALLY HAWAIIAN GIFT GALLERY

The work of over 75 of the best artists and crafts people that we have to offer. High quality gifts, art, quilts and Christmas ornaments in all price ranges, "Made with Aloha". Traditional, decorative, original items from Hawaii. **667-2558**

EDO JAPAN

Fresh ingredients cooked in front of you. Specializing in quick service teppanyaki-style dishes. Also serving sushi, noodles, specialty rice bowls, and vegetable dishes. Open daily 10:30am-9pm. No reservations needed. **661-7784**

GROOVE 2 MUSIC

Conveniently located next to Center Stage is this independently-owned music store where you're treated like an old friend, not just another customer. Records, tapes, CDs and Hawaiian Instruments. Shop online at groove2music.com. **661-4101**

FREE! *Weekly Hula Shows*

KEIKI HULA — Sat. & Sun. 1 pm
POLYNESIAN DANCERS — Tue. & Thurs. 7 pm

50 Shops • Dining & International Food Court • Fully Air-Conditioned • Free Parking
Mall Hours: 9:30 am - 9:00 pm • 1221 Honoapiilani Hwy.
Call 661-5304 for more information • www.lahainacannerymall.com
Events subject to change without notice.

LAHAINA CANNERY MALL

is this winning combination that makes shopping at any of our locations truly paradise! Map page 68. Ad on inside front cover.

GROOVE 2 MUSIC
Lahaina Cannery Mall, Lahaina.
(808) 661-4101
Website: www.groove2music.com
West Maui's location for authentic Hawaiian musical instruments and hula supplies from grass skirts to handcrafted koa wood ukuleles. Also featured is a wide selection of music to browse through, from Pop to Jazz and an extensive collection of Hawaiian music to choose from. Listening stations are available to help those who are unfamiliar with the music of Hawaii and the staff will treat you like an old friend, not just another customer, in assisting you with your selections. And for you L.P. collectors, there's a section of well kept used vinyl as well as new records. So stop by and visit, talk story, and check out the pictures of local and national musicians that make this store their stop when on Maui. You can shop online for all types of music at www.groove2music.com. Map page 68; ad page 45.

HANA FLOWER COMPANY
Toll Free 1-800-952-4262
Grower and shipper of Fresh Cut Hawaiian Flowers. Located in the rainforests of Maui, the best growing conditions in the world! Our gift boxes are shipped overnight via FedEx. Visit our website: www.hanaflowers.com for our wide variety of flowers and Hawaiian gifts. Or call us at 800-952-4262. Freshness guaranteed! Free shipping! Map page 15, ad page 104

HAWAII EXPERIENCE THEATER GIFT SHOP
824 Front St., Lahaina
(808) 661-7111
The Hawaii Experience Dome Theater also has one of Maui's favorite gift shops. Customers return year after year to browse the wide selection of clothing, jewelry, books, toys and unique gift items. Because of the wide variety of gifts at reasonable prices, many island residents as well as visitors do their gift shopping at The Hawaii Experience Theater Gift Shop. Gift shop customers earn free tickets to the Hawaii Experience 70mm movie adventure "Hawaii: Islands of the Gods" — for every $25 you spend in the gift shop you'll receive one free movie ticket, up to four tickets for a purchase of $100 or more. Map page 68; ad page 61.

HAWAIIAN QUILT COLLECTION
The Kapalua Shops
118 Bay Drive, Kapalua
(808) 665-1111 • 1-800-367-9987
Website: www.hawaiian-quilts.com
Hawaiian quilts are totally hand-made with over a million stitches and more than 1,000 hours of workmanship to complete. This Hawaiian time-honored family tradition can become your tradition as well. Our shops offer a breathtaking array of bed quilts, wall hangings, cushion covers, kits, patterns and much more. In Waikiki – Hyatt Regency and The Royal Hawaiian Hotel; On Maui – at Kapalua Shops, and our largest store at Ala Moana Center, 3rd Floor. Call us at 1-800-367-9987. Map page 81, ad page 83.

KAPALUA DISCOVERY CENTER
The Kapalua Shops, Kapalua
Located at the Kapalua Shops, The Discovery Center is a fascinating glimpse into the island's culture, environment and history. Featured displays include a photographic exhibit of Hawaii's endangered species; historical photos and stories from the Plantation Days era at Kapalua; information on Pu'u Kukui Preserve rainforest; and Hawaiian artifacts. The Discovery Center is open from 10am to 5pm daily. Admission is free. Map page 81.

THE KAPALUA LOGO SHOPS
109 Bay Drive, Kapalua
(808) 669-4172
The distinctive Kapalua butterfly adorns a fine array of fashions and accessories for family and home. At The Kapalua Logo Shop, you'll find casual and elegant resort attire for any time of the day or night. For men, there are aloha shirts, active and beach wear. For women, short sets, classic ensembles, active wear and beach accessories are perfect for vacation but travel back to your year-round wardrobe with ease.

Don't forget to visit Kapalua Kids for that special keiki in your life. You'll find the delightful butterfly on outfits and accessories for infants to size 6X. Or choose from a quality selection of toys and books to make learning fun!

Kapalua Designs is our third shop, catering to home fashions and specialty food products created especially for the Kapalua

La Perle

A unique collection of exotic natural-color pearl jewelry that connoisseurs should not miss!

• Tahitian Black, South Seas Natural-Color Pearls
• Fine selection of designer gemstone jewelry
• 14K gold jewelry featuring the exclusive Kapalua Butterfly Logo

Kapalua Shops, Kapalua
(808) 669-8466
Adjacent to the Kapalua Bay Hotel
Ample free parking • Open 9am-6pm daily

lifestyle. Bags, glassware, office accessories, golf gear and custom gift baskets are just a few of the charming items you'll discover.

Celebrate mind, body and spirit at the Kapalua Body & Bath store. A wonderful array of body products including terry and cotton robes, loofah products, aromatherapy gifts, Kapalua's own brand of creams and lotions and home accessories such as pillows, lamps and decorative bath items are available. Map page 81; ad page 82.

THE KAPALUA SHOPS
Adjacent to the Kapalua Bay Hotel

When you're looking for something a little different, Kapalua Shops has just the thing. Not your ordinary collection of stores, this eclectic grouping of boutiques and galleries has acquired a truly unique merchandise selection. The Kapalua Logo Shops, which includes Kapalua Kids and Kapalua Body & Bath, and Kapalua Designs, feature the distinctive Kapalua butterfly adorning a fine array of fashions and accessories. La Perle specializes in fabulous white and golden South Seas pearls, fashionable Tahitian black pearls, as well as sapphires, rubies, emeralds and diamonds. Lahaina Gallery at Kapalua has represented the finest of contemporary art for over nineteen years, including Raymond Page, Robert Lyn Nelson, Andrea Smith, Guy Buffet, Bill Mack, and The Turnbulls. South Seas Trading Post is one of the most interesting galleries on Maui. The McKelveys travel from the high Himalayas down to the South Seas in search of unusual and unique, one-of-a-kind items. All in all, there are over twenty distinctive shops with trinkets and treasures from around the globe. Map page 81; ad page 82.

KIHEI KALAMA VILLAGE
1941 S. Kihei Road
Across from Kalama Park
(808) 879-6610

A favorite destination for local residents and visitors. This inviting Hawaiian plantation setting is a one-stop eclectic mix of shops and theme restaurants for the whole family to enjoy. Over 40 shops feature an unusual and appealing selection of gifts, crafts and souvenirs. A variety of 10 restaurants serves breakfast, lunch, dinner and tropical drinks daily at reasonable prices. Menus items include Mexican, Greek, Thai, local entrees, fresh fish, salads, sandwiches and burgers. Ample free parking. Map page 94; ad page 97.

LA PERLE
111 Bay Drive, Kapalua
(808) 669-8466

In Tahiti forty years ago a pearl trader gave his daughter a natural, black pearl from a Tahitian lagoon. These naturally occurring black pearls are now considered extinct. That pearl, which is scarcer than large flawless diamonds, is the "seed" that inspired Alice (pronounced "Alysse") and her husband Dwayne Bower to establish La Perle in 1979, at Kapalua.

La Perle is also a French expression, meaning "The Gem". The "Gem" being most sought after at distinctive jewelry stores on Maui is the famous Tahitian Black, Natural-Color Pearl. These pearls can have hues of beautiful colors. People who love the charm, beauty, and Aloha of Maui and Polynesia are drawn to appreciate the preciousness and natural beauty of the Tahitian Natural-Color Pearls.

Fortunately, these exotic pearls are avail-

VOTED #1 SHOP!

FUKU BONSAIS AND BIRDS AND MONKEYS, OH MY!
- **EXCLUSIVE RETAILER OF FUKU-BONSAI (TRUE INDOOR TROPICAL BONSAI/EASY CARE)**
- **ADOPT A BABY BIRD - READY FOR EXPORT!**
- **ORCHIDS & ANTHURIUMS**
- **TROPICAL & EXOTIC PLANTS**
- **REGISTERED POT BELLY PIGS**
- **PLUMERIA PLANTS**
- **A FUN PLACE TO VISIT**
- **A LEGEND IN LAHAINA**
- **ALL APPROVED FOR EXPORT - MAIL ORDER AVAILABLE**
- **CELEBRATING OVER 20 YEARS OF QUALITY SERVICE!**

DAN'S GREENHOUSE

133 PRISON STREET
LAHAINA, HI 96761
(808) 661-8412
1/2 BLOCK UP FROM
LAHAINA BANYAN TREE

able today mainly due to one man's quest to farm the "Pinctada Margaritifera" oysters and to assist nature to form these exotic pearls. This entrepreneur and other pearl farmers are the sources for La Perle's "Gems of Polynesia". If you love Polynesia and some of its rarest, natural treasures visit La Perle and their "no ka oi" collection of pearls. They are "The Best" of Maui. Map page 81; ad page 46 and 83.

LAHAINA CANNERY MALL
1221 Honoapiilani Hwy, Lahaina
Through decades past, West Maui's roots in the dynamic pineapple industry can still be experienced today. Less than a mile from Lahaina harbor, tons of the exotic, succulent fruit were once processed and canned at the historic Baldwin Packers pineapple cannery, now home to Lahaina Cannery Mall and its fifty shops and restaurants. Newly renovated and climate controlled for your shopping and dining comfort, Maui's only enclosed, fully air-conditioned shopping complex gives you a taste of the pineapple industry's yesteryear. Remnants and displayed mementos of the early 1900's pineapple cannery bring the

spirit and energy of times past to life. As you stroll through the tropical-decored interior and sip your complimentary pineapple juice, explore the diversity of stores including: art galleries; book, music and toy retailers; fashion apparel, accessory and jewelry shops; specialty and Hawaiian product vendors, recreation, travel and service providers; convenience, drug and grocery stores. For a leisurely meal, relax in one of the full-service restaurants. Or, for a quick bite, stop by the food court, aptly named "Pineapple Court," and try a variety of international and local selections. While you dine, you may catch one of the many free shows on the center stage. From children's hula shows and Polynesian revues, to contemporary island music and ethnic performances, Lahaina Cannery Mall's center stage has become a meeting place for enjoyable entertainment. Melding the vibrance of current-day Maui with its treasured past, Lahaina Cannery Mall is Maui's most unique shopping paradise. Map page 68; ad pages 44 and 45.

LAHAINA GALLERIES
728 Front St., Lahaina • (808) 667-2152
The Shops at Kapalua • (808) 669-0202
The Shops at Wailea • (808) 874-8583
Website: www.lahainagalleries.com
Established in 1976, Lahaina Galleries features sculptures, paintings, and prints by renowned artists such as Charles Bragg, Guy Buffet, Dario Campanile, Ivan Clarke, Lau Chun, Frederick Hart, Aldo Luongo, Richard MacDonald, Ronaldo Macedo, Otsuka, Jan Parker, Adolf Sehring, Andrea Smith, Gary Swanson, and Robert Watson. Visit us at three convenient locations, or visit our on-line gallery at www.lahainagalleries.com. Map pages 69, 76, 94; ad page 7.

LAHAINA MOTORCYCLE WORKS
Lahaina Cannery Mall, Lahaina
(808) 661-6603
Maui's best selection of Harley-Davidson® tee-shirts. Exciting Maui and Hawaiian themes. Gift ideas galore, including his and hers gold watches, carefully crafted in Black Hills gold. Take a Harley Aloha shirt home. Better yet, get one for yourself and one for a friend. The legend goes on at Lahaina Motorcycle Works. Map page 68; ad page 44.

LOCAL MOTION
1295 Front St., Lahaina • (808) 661-7873
Lahaina Center, Lahaina • (808) 669-7873
Kaahumanu Ctr, Kahului • (808) 871-7873
Kukui Mall, Kihei • (808) 879-7873
Local Motion is Hawaii's favorite surf shop! They have the largest selection of contemporary clothing which best represents the Hawaiian surf lifestyle. It's also the best place to start your adventure into the sport of surfing. Top-quality surfboards and equipment are available for sale or rent, and the friendly staff can advise you on where to find the best surf to match your abilities. Visit one of their four convenient locations on Maui and find out why Local Motion is Hawaii's favorite surf shop. Map pages 14, 68, and 94. Ad page 113.

LOST WORLD ARTS
1036 Limahana Place, Lahaina
(808) 661-0076
Website: www.lostworldarts.com
A visit to the Lost World Arts gallery is an unforgettable experience. On display you will discover a collection of primitive art and photography from the most remote and inaccessible parts of the world. Brothers Karl and Andrew Lehmann have explored every continent but Antarctica to gather this exot-

C. ARNOLD BUILDING DESIGNS
CUSTOM HOME PLANS

Computer-Aided Design
Customer Satisfaction
Plotting In-House
Affordable Prices
Quality Work
Great Service

C. Arnold Building Designs supplies all of your architectural drafting needs from restaurant layout, drawings for committee decisions to complete home plans, condominium remodels and commercial space. We will meet with you on-site to discuss layout and design to better utilize the full potential of your property.

(808) 669-4439 • Fax: 669-0037
P.O. Box 10669, Lahaina, HI 96761 • email: homeplan4u@aol.com
http://hometown.aol.com/homeplan4u/drafting.html

SHOPS & GALLERIES

ic collection and are happy to share their experiences. They offer a selection of unique pieces, each personally collected during their expeditions, as well as incredible photographs from all parts of the globe. Visit the gallery at 1036 Limahana Place or call 661-0076 for an appointment at your convenience. Map page 68; ad page 49.

MAUI COFFEE ROASTERS
444 Hana Hwy., Kahului
(808) 877-2877 • Fax: (808) 871-2684
Toll free: 1-800-645-2877
Website: www.hawaiiancoffee.com
Why is Maui Coffee Roasters so popular? It's because this family-owned business roasts and brews some of the best coffee on Maui. Add the best coffee prices on the island and you start to see why residents and visitors alike flock to this unique caffeine oasis. Kona, along with selected coffees from Maui, Kauai and Molokai, are fresh roasted daily. They also have a savory food selection. It ranges from the ultimate veggie burger to lunch specials of Hawaiian lobster and fresh Hawaiian fish. Whether you're on the isle of Maui or at home, Maui Coffee Roasters will ship to you. Ordering couldn't be simpler... use their toll-free number, fax, email, or order from their website at www.hawaiian-coffee.com. Map page 14; ad page 49.

MAUI TREASURES
Lahaina Cannery Mall, Lahaina
Toll free: 1-800-871-0770
Direct: (808) 661-1131
Website: www.hawaiiangift.com
Email: Sales@hawaiiangift.com
Located in the Lahaina Cannery Mall, Maui Treasures carries fine quality arts and sculptures, collection jewelry, Hawaiian products, T-shirts and more at affordable prices. It's your one-stop shop to find the most unique gifts to take home from Maui. Map page 68; ad page 44.

NAPILI PLAZA
5095 Napilihau St., Napili Plaza
Looking for great stores, great values and a convenient, friendly neighborhood shopping outlet, where locals and visitors shop? Then Napili Plaza is the place to be! Let us fill your picnic baskets for a day at the beach, stock your refrigerator with local produce, dry clean your clothes and even stuff your luggage with treasures from Maui. Napili Plaza, where the merchants welcome you with real aloha. Map page 81; ad page 79.

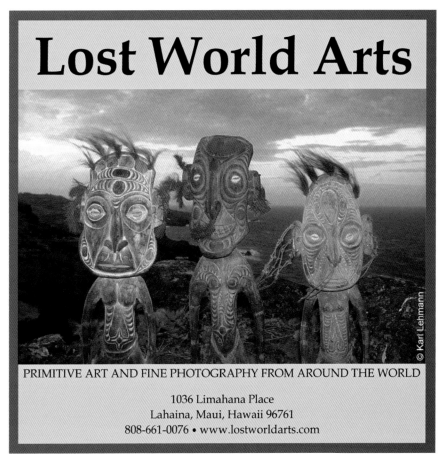

PIONEER INN SHOPS
Best Western Pioneer Inn
Corner of Front Street/Banyan Tree
and Hotel Street, Lahaina.
(808) 661-3636
This whaling inn and shopping arcade is situated on the wharf and the focal point of the Lahaina Historical District, located at the site of the first lighthouse in the Pacific. The Pioneer Inn, Hawaii's second oldest hotel, is registered by the Library of Congress. Not only is the 97-year-old Pioneer Inn surrounded by many attractions including all recreational marine activities, the Banyan tree, and the whaling ship Carthaginian, but it houses 18 of the most unique shops and merchants on Front Street. You can purchase tickets for island activities from whale watching to luaus at the Lahaina Ticket Company. When you return, have your photos processed by Kodak at Fox Photo's 1-Hour Lab while you browse for jewelry, Hawaiian gifts, clothing, art, and that special souvenir at Whaler's General Store, Maui Island Style, Leola's Family Funware, Beside the Banyan, Maui Lifestyle, Lily Boutique, Watch-N-See, Products of Hawaii Too, Fundimensional Gallery, Del Sol Sunpowered Products, Paradise Lahaina and Tidepool Gallery. Treat yourself to a cool and refreshing ice cream treat from Haagen Dazs or, for a full meal, try the Pioneer Inn's restaurants and bar. If you have a limited time to spend in Lahaina, spend it at the Historic Pioneer Inn. Map page 69; ad inside back cover.

ROLAND'S SHOES
Lahaina Cannery Mall, Lahaina
(808) 661-8114
Maui Mall, Kahului • (808) 871-4571
Azeka Place II, Kihei • (808) 879-5747
Give your feet a vacation! Roland's Shoes, serving Maui's footwear needs for the entire family since 1957. Conveniently located in Kahului at Maui Mall, Kihei at Azeka's Place II, and in Lahaina at the Lahaina Cannery Mall. Featuring popular brands including Cole Haan, Birkenstock, Teva, Sperry Top Sider, Bass, Rockport, Skechers, Onex, SAS. We also carry Hawaiian brands, including Island Slipper and Scott Hawaii. Map pages 14, 68 and 94; ad page 45.

ROXANA'S HAIR AFFAIR
5095 Napilihau Street, Napili
(808) 669-7743
Roxana's Hair Affair is a full service beauty salon located in the Napili Plaza. At Roxana's we keep ourselves on the cutting edge, always

learning new styles and using the best professional products to enhance your looks. Residents and visitors alike love to come in and get pampered by our knowledgeable and friendly staff. You can trust us to be your salon away from home. The owner, Roxana, and her husband, Captain Virgil, have three beautiful children. April 2000 will be fourteen years helping Maui's community look it's best. Open Mon-Fri 9am-6pm; Sat 9am-5pm. Map page 81; ad page 79.

THE SHOPS AT WAILEA
3750 Wailea Alanui, Wailea
Website: www.shopsatwailea.com
Located in the heart of the exclusive Wailea resort community, The Shops at Wailea is where fashion meets fantasy. Open in fall 2000, this extraordinary 150,000 square-foot retail center is the place to find everything from European and American designer fashions to Hawaiian art and collectibles. Featuring two levels of luxury, lifestyle, and specialty shops along with restaurants from casual to elegant, The Shops at Wailea is turly a shopper's paradise. A central gathering plaza with fountains, lush tropical plants and entertainment provides a comfortable, inviting oasis in which to relax between visiting shops. Parking is abundant, but you can also catch a trolly or even walk from your hotel to get to the center, which is adjacent to the Outrigger Wailea Resort and the Grand Wailea Resort Hotel and Spa™. Map page 94; ad pages 51 and 95.

ANDREA SMITH
AND MATTHEW SMITH, ARTISTS
Lahaina Galleries • 1-800-228-2006
Email: asfaltd@aol.com
Andrea Smith works in her outdoor studio inspired by the unspoiled peaks of the West Maui mountains. Smith works in mixed media, reveling in the spontaneity of water-based paints and pastels on hand made paper. Using gouache, acrylics, pastels and watercolors simultaneously, Smith allows the work to flow out of her inner consciousness. "Through my painting, the actual process, I learn a lot about life. I learn about letting everything flow, not trying too hard, letting it all come through rather than trying to control everything." As a result of this process, Andrea has created a special watercolor workshop entitled "Square One – a metaphor for life®." If you would like to know more about this special project, please call 1-800-369-1205. Lahaina Galleries invites you to come experience the peace,

harmony and joy of Andrea's paintings and sculpture. Smith paintings are in the collections of such notables as Mrs. A. Sadat, Rinaldo Brutuco (founder, World Business Academy), Roger Clemens, Mr & Mrs. M. Gorbachev, Mr. Gerald Jampolsky, Shirley Maclaine, plus many more. Matthew Smith's images are spiritual architecture, maintaining a wonderful balance and visual harmony in his paintings and works primarily in acrylics. Map pages 69 and 81; ad page 43.

TIFFANY & CO.
Whaler's Village, 2435 Kaanapali Pkwy.,
Lahaina, Maui • (808) 667-7899
Soon at The Shops at Wailea
Ala Moana Center, 1450 Ala Moana
Blvd., Honolulu • (808) 943-6677
Sheraton Moana Surfrider, 2365
Kalakaua Ave., Waikiki • (808) 926-2600
Hilton Hawaiian Village, 2005 Kalia Rd.,
Honolulu • (808) 941-7888
For more than 160 years, Tiffany & Co. has proudly presented the finest jewelry, including Jean Schlumberger, Elsa Peretti and Paloma Picasso. In addition, Tiffany & Co. is a purveyor of quality timepieces, china, crystal, silver, stationery, accessories, and fragrances. Tiffany & Co. has three locations on Oahu and two locations on Maui at Whalers Village and The Shops at Wailea. Open daily. Map page 76 and 94; ad page 5.

TOTALLY HAWAIIAN GIFT GALLERY
Lahaina Cannery Mall, Lahaina
(808) 667-2558
High quality gifts, authentic Hawaiian crafts, and sterling silver or 14k gold jewelry displayed in a friendly, well-designed store. A large selection of Koa bowls, Ni'ihau Shell Leis, and hand-stitched Hawaiian style quilt, pot holders, pillows and bedspreads are some of the unique products available here. Often told that his selection is "nicer than other stores," Jeff Blayer spends much of his time choosing the best that the island's artists have to offer. Doll collectors appreciate his selection of porcelain, bear and Tutu handcrafted dolls. Tea towels to trivets and a year-round selection of Christmas ornaments are some of the gifts available from the store where the locals shop. Recommended for gourmet and wine accessories. Open 7 days a week 9:30am to 9:00pm. Map page 68; ad page 45.

The Shops at Wailea

Your Place In The Sun

A shopper's paradise in the heart of the exclusive Wailea Resort, featuring two levels of luxury, lifestyle and specialty shops along with restaurants from casual to elegant. *Open in Fall 2000.*

3750 Wailea Alanui, Wailea, Maui, Hawaii
For leasing information phone (808) 524-3551
www.shopsatwailea.com

MAUI DISCOVERIES

Totally Hawaiian Gift Gallery. Maui's most distinctive gift shop has a complete selection of gifts from hand-stitched quilts to one-of-a-kind dolls. We specialize in hand-crafted koa wood bowls, Hawaiian Christmas ornaments, and other high-quality gifts. Located in the Lahaina Cannery Mall. See page 45.

▼

▲

Celebrate Mind, Body & Spirit at **Kapalua Body & Bath**, located at the Kapalua Shops. Botanicals, lotions, aromatherapy and spa gifts as well as lounge and resortwear adorned with the Kapalua butterfly logo. See page 83.

◄ One-stop shopping and dining for the entire family: check out the popular **Garys Island** for the finest in aloha wear for men, women and kids. See inside front cover.

Head for the seaside dining at **Woody's Oceanfront Grill**, featuring steak, seafood, chicken and ribs. See page 27. ►

MAUI DISCOVERIES

"As a 'plain air' landscape painter, the endless variety and quantity of beauty here is, at times, overwhelming! This informal garden had caught my eye several times. The radiance of the bougainvillea and surrounding flowers seemed to color the air. This wonderful feeling of exuberance and 'pink air' was my stimulus and goal for this painting." —Leonard Wren. "Hawaiian Blush" is available at **Collectors Fine Art of Hawaii** located in the Hyatt Regency Hotel, Kaanapali, Maui. See page 3.

La Perle is your best source for the immensely popular natural-color pearls from French Polynesia, known as Tahitian Black Pearls. Visit **La Perle** and see their collection featuring rare pearls with exotic hues handcrafted into fabulous jewelry in 18K gold. See page 46 and 83.

"Saturday Evening" by Aldo Luongo is available at **Lahaina Galleries** in Lahaina, The Shops at Kapalua, and The Shops at Wailea. See page 7.

The Hawaii Experience Domed Theater also features one of Maui's most popular gift shops, featuring clothing, toys, jewelry, books, and many unusual items for all ages. First-time and repeat visitors alike consider this the perfect place to pick up mementoes of their trip to Maui for themselves or for friends back home. Receive one movie ticket free with every $25 purchase ($6.95 value; maximum 4 tickets with $100 purchase). See page 61.

MAUI DISCOVERIES

This rare Black Palm Cockatoo "Prince Ele Ele" is just one of the many exotic birds available for adoption and export at **Dan's Greenhouse**. You can also take Fuku Bonsai Trees and other tropical plants home, or a certified pot belly pig. See page 47.

Let **Roxana's Hair Affair** create the look you want on your special day. Our professional hair and nail staff will put the finishing touch on that memorable occasion. See page 79.

"**Best Of Maui**" is a beautiful reminder of your trip to Maui. Features the most current, up-to-date guide about what to do and see on Maui, illustrated by high-quality color photography. Updated annually. 8 1/2" x 11", hard cover, 128pp, $15. See order form between pages 132 and 133, or mail payment to Sandwich Islands Publishing, P.O. Box 10669, Lahaina, HI 96761.

Hula implements and Hawaiian instruments, handcrafted here on Maui, are available at **Groove 2 Music**, along with a wide selection of Hawaiian music. Located at the Lahaina Cannery Mall. See page 45.

"**Maui On My Mind**" is the best-selling, full color, award-winning must buy for anyone who loves Maui. This unique collection of landscapes, aerials, action sports, people, underwater scenes and vintage photos support a narrative text telling the story of Maui from its fiery volcanic birth. Large format 11" x 14", hard cover, 256 pp, color and 45 rare historical photos. $49 includes air mail postage. See order form between pages 132 and 133, or mail payment to Sandwich Islands Publishing, P.O. Box 10669, Lahaina, HI 96761.

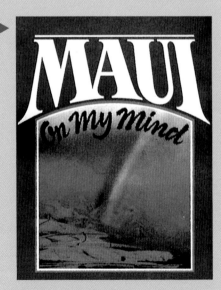

MAUI DISCOVERIES

"Woman Coming Down from the Wall" George's experience at Dunhuang Cave was the basis for this work. The statues and large wall paintins all around him gave the impression of "real beauties coming down from the stonewall, glowing and shining!" He proceeded to cast a large mask – symbolizing the guardian, the observer, the master. Available at Collectors Fine Art of Hawaii located in the Hyatt Regency Hotel, Kaanapali, Maui. See page 3.

DFS Galleria Maui is the place to shop at Whaler's Village Shopping Center in Kaanapali. Visitors and locals alike will discover unique gifts including Hawaiian jewelry, local surf wear and gourmet island foods. For international travelers, enjoy the finest name-brand duty-free merchandise from around the world. See directory listing on page 42.

MONICA STEVENSON

Tiffany & Co., world-renowned for the highest quality diamonds, introduces Lucida™, an exclusive new diamond cut and ring setting. The new diamond cut is a square mixed-cut with a high step-cut crown, wide corners, and a brilliant-style pavilion that reveal the stone's inner sparkle and brilliance. Inspired by a combination of two period facetting styles, this new cut is a pure and modern expression of contemporary taste. See ad on page 5.

Hawaiian Quilt Collection: Beautiful hand-made Hawaiian quilts, pillows, wall hangings, kits and much more. We pamper those who are "Hawaiian at Heart". Visit us on the internet: www.Hawaiian-Quilts.com. See ad on page 83.

ISLAND ACTIVITIES

A directory of the most exciting activities Maui has to offer

ACTIVE VOLCANO AIR TOURS
(808) 877-5500
Website: www.maui.net/~mauisle
Email: volcanotour@maui.net
Maui and its neighboring islands are best seen from the air as the vast majority of each island is inaccessible from the ground. One of the best values on Maui is the active volcano air tour of Maui and the Big Island of Hawaii in one of Volcano Air Tour's comfortable, air-conditioned, twin-engine, ten seat airplanes. Each passenger has their own large window in two abreast seating and a stereo headset for music and expert pilot narration. See waterfalls, steep cliffs, rain forests and Madam Pele's current activity at the world's most active volcano. Volcano Air Tours is the only fixed-wing air tour company on Maui, with air-conditioned airplanes and the most experience flying tours of the islands with a per-

fect safety record and FAA certified. Departures from both West Maui Kapalua airport and Kahului airport. Limited seats make reservations necessary, so call their friendly reservationist between 7am and 9pm anyday with your credit card number early in your vacation. Map pages 14 and 81. Ad page 56.

ALEXAIR HELICOPTERS
(808) 871-0792
Close your eyes and visualize the Maui you have always dreamed of. Witness the dramatic beauty of our lush tropical rainforests, cascading waterfalls and magical Haleakala Crater, our dormant volcano. Take a tour that lands on an exclusive black sand beach for a picnic. We provide a variety of tours designed to fit any family size or budget. Soar through the Maui skies in one of our Starships designed specifically for touring. All aircraft have

two-way communication which provides for a more informative flight. Most flights come with a complimentary video. Map page 14; ad page 117.

BE MARRIED ON MAUI
Reverand Susan Osborn
2162 Kahookele Street, Wailuku, HI 96793
(808) 244-7400; toll free 1-888-542-9520
http://www.maui.net/~revsuzio/wedding.htm
Email: revsuzio@maui.net
"All You Need is Love" "Rev. Suzi O" offers Romantic, Spiritual and Affordable Wedding, Vow Renewals or Commitment Ceremonies. The most important thing in selecting someone to assist you as your marriage officiant and wedding coordinator, besides their being efficient and professional of course, is whether you'll enjoy working with them. Even though your ceremony is a solemn occasion, I do what I can to make it fun during the entire planning process. I love my job — I get to work with people who are happy, in love and excited to be getting Married on Maui. Short notice ceremonies are not a problem!! Call me or E me...!

EMBASSY VACATION RESORTS KAANAPALI
140 Kaanapali Shores Place
(808) 661-2000
Welcome to the Suite Life. Embassy Vacation Resort is located beach front on Maui's magnificent north Kaanapali Beach, overlooking the crystal blue Pacific and the lush green mountains of West Maui. The luxurious 12-story all-suite resort is right where you want to be -- close to attractions, beaches and conveniences; but far away from life's worries. It is here that you will discover the comfort and service of a first-class hotel combined with the independence and easy living of a finely appointed condominium. The one-acre swimming pool with water slide is a wonderful place for fun all day. Or take to beach for snorkeling, scuba diving, sailing, or just soaking up the island sun in private cabana. When the day is done, you'll see why this resort is the recipient of the coveted RCI Gold Crown Award. Map page 76; ad page 23.

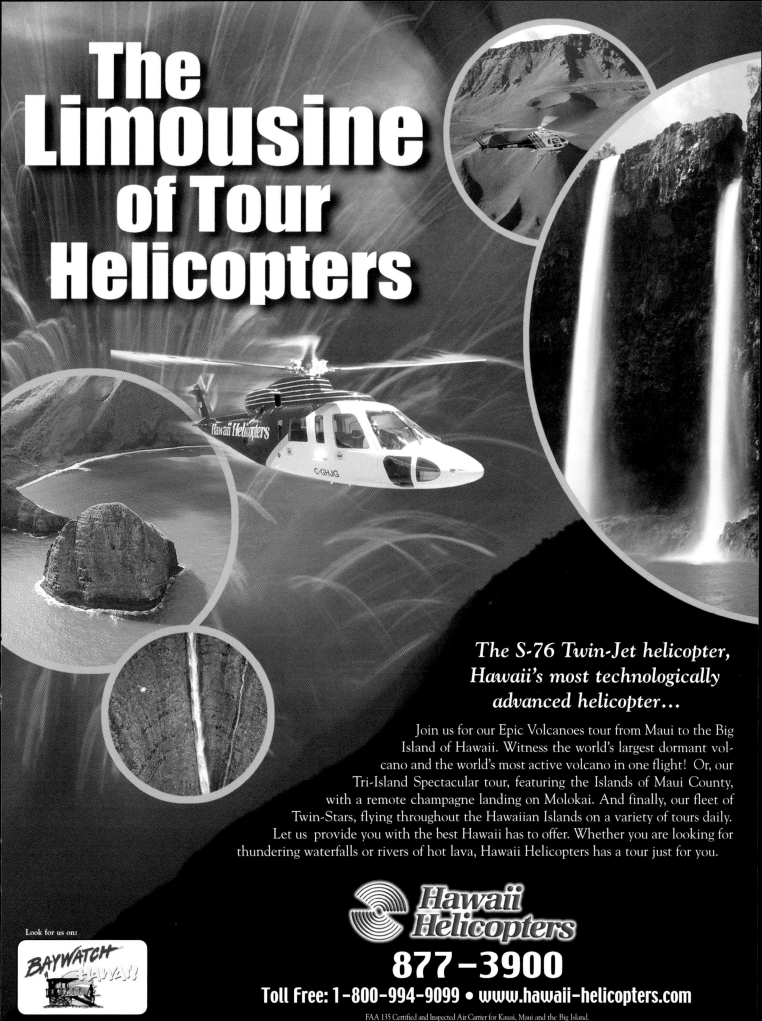

EXPEDITIONS

(808) 661-3756

Traveling to Lana'i is easy and fun when you book passage on Expeditions, with 5 round-trips daily from Lahaina Harbor, Maui and Manele Harbor, Lana'i. Two of the top-rated golf courses in the world are on Lana'i and golf packages can be arranged. Hawaii's most secluded island, Lana'i, also offers two luxury resorts with packages available through Expeditions. Additionally, cars, jeeps, and island tours can be booked, or pack a lunch and explore on your own. The incredible Hulopoe Marine Preserve is only a 10-minute walk from Manele Harbor on Lana'i, so take your snorkel gear. Call us for reservations so that you may enjoy this beautiful private isle at your leisure. Map page 69; ad page 91.

THE FEAST AT LELE

Beachside at 505 Front Street

(808) 667-5353

From the originators of Hawai'i's most authentic and award-winning lū'au, Old Lāhaina Lū'au, and the creators of two of Hawai'i's best restaurants, pacific'O and i'o, comes a new concept in cultural celebration. Opened in April 1999, The Feast at Lele is already on its way to becoming one of Hawai'i's premier attractions. In an intimate beachside setting, guests enjoy a lavish culinary, dramatic and musical voyage through the Island nations of Hawai'i, Tonga, Tahiti, and Samoa. The spectacular grounds are also available for weddings and vow renewal ceremonies, creating memories sure to last a lifetime. The Feast at Lele is presented every Tuesday, Wednesday, Thursday and Saturday. Map page 69, ad page 35.

HANNA SOMATICS EDUCATION

(808) 879-2227

There are fifty-four certified Hanna Somatic Educators® on the planet. One resides on Maui. What is Hanna Somatic Education? It's a breakthrough modality which reverses chronic pain and stiffness resulting from injuries, surgeries or accumulated stress. This method employs movement education to awaken body awareness, re-establish voluntary muscular control and rejuvenate function. Guided by Cynthia Lindway, your private Somatics Lesson will consist of an initial evaluation to determine appropriate strategy tailored to your needs. Unlike other modalities, you remain fully-clothed. Rather than having something done to you or for you, Cynthia works with you, therefore a lasting change is made. What you learn during a Somatics Lesson is how to regain conscious control of your muscles. Re-educated muscles do not hurt; movement is smoother and freer. As a result, you will move more comfortably, increase your flexibility, enjoy more energy, obtain stress management skills, improve athletic skills, regain balance, improve posture, and age with comfort, flexibility and grace. Ad page 97.

HAWAII HELICOPTERS

(808) 877-3900 • 1-800-994-9099

Website: www.hawaii-helicopters.com

We are the only company in Hawaii offering the added safety and peace of mind of Twin Engine helicopters. Serving Hawaii for over 15 years, Hawaii Helicopters offers a variety of tours including our exclusive Epic Volcanoes Tour and our Tri-Island Spectacular Tour. Witness the World's largest dormant volcano and the World's most active volcano in one flight, or, tour the islands of Maui, Lanai and Molokai with a remote champagne landing on Molokai at Kalaupapa Peninsula. Our pilots are State Certified Tour Guides that leave each passenger with better knowledge of Hawaii's rich history. Whether you are interested in

RON DAHLQUIST

seeing rivers of hot bubbling lava, isolated waterfalls plummeting thousands of feet into remote pools, or rain forests untouched by man, Hawaii Helicopters has a tour just for you. Indulge yourself! Map page 14; ad page 57.

THE HAWAII EXPERIENCE DOMED THEATER

824 Front Street, Lahaina
(808) 661-8314

Take a magic carpet tour of the Islands via a 70mm projection on a 60-foot domed screen with an eight-channel surround sound system. This million-dollar production, Hawaii, Islands of the Gods, showcases the Islands' natural beauty, wildlife and marine environments. Viewers "fly" over erupting volcanoes and "swim" alongside humpback whales while relaxing in the safety and comfort of a planetarium seat in the air-conditioned theater. The theater lobby is also one of Maui's best gift shops, featuring clothing, toys, jewelry, books, and many unusual items for all ages. This is the perfect place to pick up momentoes of your trip to Maui, or as a gift for that special friend back home. Gift shop customers earn free tickets to the Hawaii Experience 70mm movie adventure "Hawaii: Islands of the Gods" — for every $25 you spend in the gift shop you'll receive one free movie ticket, up to four tickets for a purchase of $100 or more. The theater and gift shop are open daily with hourly film showings from 10am till 10pm. Map page 68; ad on page 61.

IRONWOOD RANCH

(808) 669-4991

View a romantic sunset the way it was meant to be seen — on horseback! Ironwood Ranch offers remote trails through tropical valleys and has scenic coastal views. The ranch offers convenient hotel pick up from West Maui resorts and is located in the North-West Maui mountains. All riding levels are welcome. You will be matched with a well-groomed mount, appropriate to your experience, from our individually-selected horses. Call 669-4991 for a reservation today. All rides are guided. Map page 81; ad pages86 and 59.

KAANAPALI GOLF COURSES

Kaanapali Resort
Pro Shop: (808) 661-3691
Driving Range: (808) 667-7111

The Kaanapali Golf Courses, Tournament North designed by Robert Trent Jones, Sr. and the Resort South designed by Arthur Jack Snyder, offer you the very best of Hawaii's unique golf challenges. Scenic fairways, rolling greens, existing beauty with sweeping views of the ocean and mountains. These courses have hosted Shell's Wonderful World of Golf, the Canada Cup, and the Women's Kemper Open. The Tournament North Course is the site of the Kaanapali Classic, a Senior PGA Tour event. Open 7:00am daily. Located at the entrance of the Kaanapali Resort. Map page 76; ad page 65.

Enjoy The Scenery
Let us do the driving
SpeediShuttle
Affordable Door-To-Door Shuttle
Maui · Big Island
661-6667 · 1-800-977-2605
www.speedishuttle.com

Experience the Romance of a Hawaiian Sunset on Horseback at

Ironwood Ranch

CALL FOR RESERVATIONS
(808) 669-4991
日本人のお客様を歓迎いたします。

FAST FACTS
Hrs: Mon-Sat
Phone: 669-4991
See map page 33

ACTIVITIES DIRECTORY

MAUI DIVE SHOP
6 Locations Throughout Maui
(808) 879-3388 • (808) 661-6166
One of the most popular and exciting activities for all visitors to Maui is snorkeling and diving. A sport that everyone can do, snorkeling and diving offers a whole new world which most people have only dreamed about as they watch it on television. There are few places in the world that offer warm clear water, an abundance of easy accesses to reefs, and the spectacular marine life that Maui is blessed with. There are also few places in the world that can offer as complete a selection of retail merchandise, the highest quality of rental equipment, the most comprehensive instructional programs, and the spectacular variety of charter boat activities that Maui Dive shop does. Yes, Maui Dive Shop, Hawaii's largest diving retailer with 6 island locations has everything you need to explore Maui's underwater world and is right near where you are. Our extensive staff of retail sales persons, snorkeling and scuba instructors, and charter boat captains await you each day to show you the time of your life and make your dreams your personal reality. Call for the best day of your vacation. Map pages 68, 76, 81 and 94; ad page 109.

MAUI HAWAII WEDDINGS
WITH REV. MARSHA ROGERS
(808) 669-6404 • 1-800-466-6176
What a wonderful and romantic island Maui is with its enchanting ocean and sunset views. A perfect paradise to begin your journey through life together. I am Rev. Marsha Rogers, and I have been performing Hawaiian wedding and vow renewal services on Maui for many years. I am licensed by the State of Hawaii and I am a member of the Maui Wedding Association and Hawaii Visitor's and Convention Bureau. One of my greatest joys in life is joining couples in union. My personalized ceremonies come from my heart and my life experiences. My intention is to perform the most beautiful ceremony and loving service for you and your guests. I promise you a wonderful memory that will remain in your hearts forever.

MAUI MARRIOTT LUAU
Maui Marriott Hotel, Kaanapali Beach
(808) 661-LUAU (661-5828)
See listing on page 76.

MAUI MYTH & MAGIC THEATRE
"ULALENA"
(808) 661-9913
Website: mauitheatre.com
A show not to be missed out and a "feast for the senses," 'Ulalena is a blockbuster stage production which finds its roots in the myths and legends of Hawaii. Presented live at the new Maui Myth & Magic Theatre in Lahaina, 'Ulalena is an artistic tribute to the unique cultures and traditions of the Islands. The performance brings to life such elements as the surreal "birth of the islands", delightful fish puppets, the unleashing of Pele's dramatic fury and the making of magical rain. The visually stunning productions is staged live by over 25 professional performers and musicians in a state-of-the-art theatre where cutting edge technology is combined with dramatic choreography, an original musical score and stunning scenography to produce a unique theatrical experience. A treat for both young and old. 'Ulalena is performed twice nightly/five days a week. For reservations call (808) 661-9913 or visit our website at mauitheatre.com. Map page 68, ad page 22.

MAUI OCEAN CENTER
Highway 30 at Ma'alaea Harbor Village
(808) 270-7000
Visitors to Maui are now able to explore Hawaii's precious and unique undersea world without ever getting wet at the Maui Ocean Center. The largest tropical aquarium in the USA, Maui Ocean Center features unique marine life found only in Hawaii. Centrally located with a spectacular view of Ma'alaea Harbor and the ocean, the park is home to thousands of indigenous fish, sharks, turtles, stingrays, and other fascinating marine animals. In the popular Underwater Journey visitors can stroll through a tunnel representing a 240-degree view of sharks and other fascinating marine life in a 750,000-gallon, open-ocean tank. Map pages 14 and 94; ad page 12 and 13.

'OHE'O STABLES
(808) 667-2222
Breathtaking views of tropical waterfalls and the old Maui that were visible everywhere before the haoles paved paradise can still be seen from horseback. 'Ohe'o Stables takes you into the only National Park area on Maui set in the tropics: 'Ohe'o Gulch of Kipahulu Valley. Trailguides rich in Hawaiian tradition and folklore are at your service. Because we take only six guests per excursion, we are available to answer your every question. Break away from the crowds. Enjoy a light breakfast at our authentic Hawaiian hale and a memorable picnic lunch high in the mountains, overlooking the incredible waimoku falls and bamboo forest. Call 'Ohe'o Stables at 667-2222. "This was definitely the high point of our vacation. Well worth the time and effort to drive out." -Rosaline & Nicholas Romano, Arizona. Map page 15; ad page 103.

OLD LĀHAINA LŪʻAU
1285 Front Street
(Oceanside of Lahaina Cannery Mall)
(808) 667-1998
The aloha flows freely seven nights a week at Hawai'i's most authentic and most award-winning lū'au, the Old Lāhaina Lū'au. A flower lei greeting, tropical drink service and imu ceremony at the water's edge begin the evening. In addition to kalua pig, you'll enjoy traditional island favorites like poke, lomi-lomi salmon and haupia. Other selections on the bountiful buffet include baked mahimahi, tropical guava chicken, teriyaki sirloin steak and all the accompaniments. The premium open bar serves all evening. After dinner, relax and enjoy the sunset while the songs and dances of old Hawai'i are presented with love and reverence, bringing alive the history, magic, and aloha of our magnificent islands. Map page 68; ad page 37.

SPEEDISHUTTLE AIRPORT SHUTTLE
(808) 661-6667 • 1-800-977-2605
www.speedishuttle.com
SpeediShuttle Airport Shuttle offers door-to-door pick up and drop off service in air-conditioned vans and buses. Sit back and enjoy the scenery in comfort

ACTIVITIES DIRECTORY

while someone else does the driving. SpeediShuttle also offers door-to-door service to Maui's most popular activities, including the heliport, all harbors, special events, golf courses, luaus, and major visitor attractions. Want to shop till you drop? SpeediShuttle can take you to all of Maui's best shopping centers, including Kaahumanu Center, Whaler's Village, Shops at Kapalua, Shops at Wailea, and more. Call for group transfers and special rates. Map page 15; ad page 59.

UFO ADVENTURES
Parasailing on Kaanapali Beach
(808) 661-7836

Soar above Maui's aqua-blue waters and take in the beauty of Maui's west side, including the islands of Lana'i and Moloka'i. May 15th to December 14th, their state-of-the-art winchboats gently lift you on and off the back of the boat for safe, dry landings. Enjoy a scenic boat ride while waiting your turn to rise skyward — solo or with a friend — spectators welcome. UFO makes parasailing safe and fun for everyone, even the physically challenged. Map page 76; ad page 61.

WAILEA'S FINEST LUAU
at the Outrigger Wailea Resort
3700 Wailea Alanui
(808) 879-1922

At the Outrigger Wailea's Finest Luau, you'll be welcomed in customary Hawaiian style with a complimentary shell lei and mai-tai or tropical fruit punch. As you watch the sun descend into the Pacific, the aroma of an authentic Hawaiian feast begins to fill the air as the *"Paradyse"* trio entertains you. When the torches are lit and the conch shell is sounded, it's time to indulge in some of the finest traditional Hawaiian food and drink in all the islands. As you finish your feast, *Paradyse* and the hula dancers share the culture, history and legends of Hawaii and Polynesia through dance and music. The evening ends with a spectacular Fire Knife Dance, which will thrill and excite visitors of all ages. Reservations suggested, 879-1922. Map page 94, ad page 96.

THE HAWAII EXPERIENCE
DOMED THEATER

70MM MOVIE ADVENTURE

Explore with us **"Hawaii: Islands of the Gods"** in a spectacular **OmniVision** motion picture experience. Voyage the Hawaiian Islands on our giant 3 story high domed screen in an unforgettable 40 minute movie adventure!

Continuous Shows On The Hour: 10am - 10pm Daily
Adults $6.95 / Children (4-12) $3.95 • 24 Hour Information Line 661-8314
VISA - MC - AMEX - JCB
Located on Lahaina's Historic Front Street • 824 Front St., Lahaina, HI 96761

PARASAIL

Soar above it all with an experienced crew and the latest in lift-off and landing technology. Fly away in ease and comfort. You may be a likely abductee. Alone or with a companion, it can happen to anybody! – The young, the old and the physically challenged.

• Atmospheric travel: 400 ft for seven minutes. **$42**

• Stratospheric travel: 800 ft. for 10 minutes. Optional simulated free fall, no extra charge. **$52**

Two can parasail together.

UFO ADVENTURES

Book Your Abduction Today!
Call Mission Control:
MAUI: 661-7UFO
KAILUA-KONA: (808) 325-5UFO

Parasailing on Maui from May 15 to December 14. Kailua-Kona Parasailing, all year 'round.

MAINLAND: 1-800-FLY-4UFO • web: www.ufoparasail.com • email: ufomaui@mauigateway.com

MAUI GOLFING TIPS

by Chris Arnold

The first hole at the Kaanapali North Course is a par 5 reachable in two shots. With water on the right, the risk may not be worth the reward. Photo courtesy of Kaanapali Golf Courses.

So, you want to play some golf on Maui? Well? do it. You're at a major destination golf resort mecca. Let me give you a few pointers before you go. Regardless if you are a 15+ handicap or you are a grinder and shoot two over most of the time, you will have to start with recognizing the grain. Most of the courses in Hawaii are bermuda grass greens. This means the grain is strong. The strain of bermuda grass greens in Japan are even stronger, that's why a lot of players in Japan chip the ball farther in the air, so they can deal with less grain. Well, Hawaii golf is along the same lines. Fly your ball farther to the hole to avoid less grain when chipping and be aware of the direction of the grain when chipping and putting. I will talk about approach shots in a bit.

When chipping, open the face a little and hit it a bit harder to the spot you want to land the ball. The opened faced lofting effect will fly the ball farther, so hence, you're dealing with less grain. On the mainland you will find more bent grass greens where you can back up a five iron from 175 yards. There are four courses in the state of Hawaii that have bent

grass greens; The Experience at Koele on the island of Lanai, Makalei Hawaiian Country Club and Big Island Country Club on the island of Hawaii, and Koolau on the island of Oahu. Of course you might want to hit that 5 iron pure to do that. Take a 4 iron just in case.

The grain always runs to the WEST. If you can figure out where the sun is going to set before you hit a chip or putt you will achieve a world of wonder. If you have a putt that looks straight and west is to the right, it will break right. I should add; the breaks are greater in the spring and summer before the grass goes dormant. Yes, the grass in Hawaii stops growing in the winter. Hard to believe, but it's true.

On the upper west side near Kapalua, west is generally between Lanai and Molokai. If somebody tells you your putts will break towards Molokai or the water, don't believe them, they probably want a piece of your pocket book in the way of skins. On the south side near Wailea and Makena west is generally between Lanai and Kaho'olawe. Also, be aware of uphill or downhill putts. If your five footer for birdie is down hill and towards the west it will be very fast. And vice-versa, an uphill putt for bogey, against the grain, east, will be very slow. If you are not sure, carry a compass. Also, it doesn't matter what you are putting for.

Approach shots? Play Hawaii golf courses as if they were links courses. I know this is contrary to what I said about chipping. They play a lot of bump and runs on links courses. You can do that effectively here in the Islands, with a good understanding of grain. Anyway, depending on your high or low trajectory you want to land the ball 10 to 20 maybe even 30 to 40 yards short of your actual distance. The ball will release on most occasions. Unless you play a balata type ball, with high spin rates, your going to have a hard time stopping the ball. Just land it short.

The Wind. I capitalize Wind because it can be a great factor here in the Islands. If you know how to hit a low, knock-down shot on command, when it is windy, do it. Most high fades, or should I say slices will be lost and gone forever. Most courses, if not all, are designed to be played in Trade Winds. These winds generally come out of the northeast and average 15 to 20 mph. From time to time we get what's called Kona winds. These winds come out of the south and can make most courses a bit more difficult. During Kona winds you will notice vog from the Big Island volcanos. Take your time, study the wind, swing easy with a 3/4 backswing, keep your balance and hit it solid. And don't forget to keep your head down.

Maui county offers a great array of spectacular courses. From Kapalua's championship courses with gentle trades to Wailea and Makena's south coast courses and across to Lanai's magnificent 36 or Molokai's Kaluakoi, you can't go wrong. The layouts and service are impeccable, the scenery inspiring. Don't let the slope or course ratings scare you. The ratings seem a bit higher in the islands, mostly because of the wind. Layout does play a big part. Just remember, this means you get more strokes compared to handicap. The only problem is this applies to your partner too.

If you want to work on your game, visit one of our local golf professionals. Enjoy!

The fifth hole at Kaanapali North is a demanding par 4 that runs along the ocean. The deep narrow green is protected by two bunkers in the front. Photo courtesy of Kaanapali Golf Courses.

GOLFING DIRECTORY

KAPALUA - THE PLANTATION COURSE		slope	rating	yardage
	Blue	142	75.2	7,263
Kapalua, Maui phone: 669-8044	White	135	71.9	6,547
stats: 64/73(75)* opened: 1991	Red	129	73.2	5,627

Resort; driving range; practice green; pro shop;
lessons; twilight rates; locker/showers;
restaurant. Ben Crenshaw/Bill Coore

KAPALUA - THE VILLAGE COURSE		slope	rating	yardage
	Blue	139	73.3	6,632
Kapalua, Maui phone: 669-8044	White	134	70.4	6,001
stats: 63/71* opened: 1981	Red	122	70.9	5,134

Resort; practice green; pro shop; lessons;
twilight rates; The Village cafe.   Arnold Palmer

KAPALUA - THE BAY COURSE		slope	rating	yardage
	Blue	138	71.7	6,600
Kapalua, Maui phone: 669-8044	White	133	69.2	6,051
stats: 62/72* opened: 1975	Red	121	69.6	5,124

Resort; driving range; practice green;
pro shop; lessons; twilight rates;
restaurant. Arnold Palmer

KAANAPALI - NORTH COURSE		slope	rating	yardage
	Champ	134	72.8	6,994
Lahaina, Maui phone: 661-3691	Regular	130	70.0	6,136
stats: 62/71* opened: 1962	Forward	123	71.1	5,417

Resort; driving range; practice green;
pro shop; lessons; twilight rates; locker/showers;
restaurant. Robert Trent Jones Sr.

KAANAPALI - SOUTH COURSE		slope	rating	yardage
	Champ	127	70.7	6,555
Lahaina, Maui phone: 661-3691	Regular	124	68.7	6,067
stats: 67/71* opened: 1976	Forward	120	69.8	5,485

Resort; driving range; practice green;
pro shop; lessons; twilight rates;
locker/showers; restaurant. Arthur Jack Snyder

SANDALWOOD GOLF COURSE		slope	rating	yardage
	Blue	129	70.6	6,469
Wailuku, Maui phone: 242-4653	White	125	68.3	6,011
stats: 66/72* opened: 1991	Red	118	64.8	5,162

Public; driving range; practice green; pro shop;
lessons; twilight rates; locker/showers;
restaurant. Nelson/Wright

THE DUNES AT MAUI LANI		slope	rating	yardage
	Black	136	73.5	6,841
Kahului, Maui phone: 873-0422	Blue	130	71.6	6,413
stats: 69/72* opened: 1999	White	121	68.3	5,833
	Red	114	67.9	4,768

Public; pro shop; twilight rates;
clubhouse Nov '99. Robin Nelson

ELLEAIR COUNTRY CLUB		slope	rating	yardage
	Gold	124	72.0	6,801
Kihei, Maui phone: 874-0777	Blue	120	70.6	6,404
stats: 62/71* opened: 1987	White	117	68.8	6,003
	Red	118	70.0	5,265

Public; driving range; practice green;
pro shop; lessons, twilight rates; restaurant. W.J. Newis

WAILEA BLUE COURSE		slope	rating	yardage
	Blue	130	71.6	6,758
Wailea, Maui phone: 879-2966	White	125	68.9	6,152
stats: 64/72* opened: 1973	Red	117	72.0	5,291

Resort; driving range; practice green; pro shop;
lessons; twilight rates; restaurant.
Aurthur Jack Snyder

WAILEA GOLD COURSE		slope	rating	yardage
	Gold	139	73.0	7,070
Wailea, Maui phone: 879-2966	Blue	136	71.4	6,653
stats: 68/72* opened: 1994	White	131	69.0	6,152
	Red	121	70.3	5,317

Resort; driving range; practice green;
pro shop; lessons; lockers/showers;
twilight rates; restaurant. Robert Trent Jones

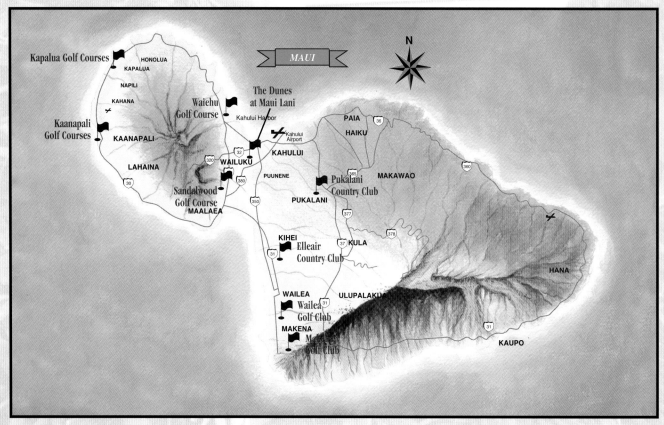

WAILEA EMERALD COURSE
Wailea, Maui phone: 879-2966
stats: 66/72* opened: 1995
Resort; driving range; practice green; pro shop; lessons; lockers/showers; twilight rates; restaurant. Robert Trent Jones

	slope	rating	yardage
Emerald	134	72.0	6,825
Blue	132	70.0	6,407
White	127	68.2	5,873
Red	119	69.5	5,268

MAKENA NORTH COURSE
Makena, Maui phone: 879-3344
stats: na/72* opened: 1986
Resort; driving range; practice green; pro shop; lessons; lockers/showers; twilight rates; restaurant. Robert Trent Jones Jr.

	slope	rating	yardage
Black	139	72.1	6,914
Blue	136	70.4	6,567
Orange	132	68.4	6,151
White	128	70.9	5,503

MAKENA SOUTH COURSE
Makena, Maui phone: 879-3344
stats: 64/72* opened: 1981/86
Resort; driving range; practice green; pro shop; lessons; lockers/showers; twilight rates; restaurant. Robert Trent Jones Jr.

	slope	rating	yardage
Black	138	72.6	7,017
Blue	134	70.7	6,629
Orange	129	68.5	6,168
White	130	71.1	5,529

PUKALANI GOLF COURSE
Pukalani, Maui phone: 572-1314
stats: na/72(74)* opened: na
Public; driving range; practice green; pro shop; lessons; restaurant.

	slope	rating	yardage
Champ	na	72.8	6,945
Regular	121	70.6	6,494
Forward	118	71.1	5,574

WAIEHU GOLF COURSE
Wailuku, Maui phone: 243-7400
stats: na/72* opened: 1930/64
Public; driving range; practice green; showers; pro shop; lessons; restaurant.

	slope	rating	yardage
White	111	69.8	6,330
Red	115	70.8	5,511

THE CHALLENGE AT MANELE
Manele Bay, Lanai phone: 565-2975
stats: 65/72* opened: 1993
Resort; driving range; practice green; pro shop; lessons; lockers/showers; nine hole rate; restaurant. Jack Nicklaus

	slope	rating	yardage
Blue	125	69.8	6310
White	122	67.8	5,847
Red	119	68.8	5,024

THE EXPERIENCE AT KOELE
Lanai City, Lanai phone: 565-4653
stats: 63/72* opened: 1991
Resort; driving range; practice green; pro shop; lessons; lockers/showers; nine hole rate; restaurant. Greg Norman/Ted Robinson

	slope	rating	yardage
Blue	134	71.5	6,626
White	130	69.7	6,217
Red	123	66.6	5,425

KALUAKOI GOLF COURSE
Maunaloa, Molokai phone: 552-2739
stats: 65/72* opened: 1977
Resort; driving range; practice green; proshop; lessons. Ted Robinson

	slope	rating	yardage
Blue	129	72.3	6,564
White	122	70.3	6,187
Red	119	71.4	5,461

IRONWOOD HILLS GOLF COURSE
Kualapuu, Molokai phone: 567-6000
stats: 61/68 opened: 1929
Private/open to public; proshop; nine holes; nine hole rate. Mr. Cook

	slope	rating	yardage
Blue	130	70.0	6,176
White	129	67.6	5,632
Red	124	68.9	4,818

Stats Information=course record/par(forward tees)

GOLF SPECIAL TEES

For tee time, call 808-661-3691.

Kaanapali Golf Courses

Visit us at www.kaanapali-golf.com

Two hundred year ago all sea roads led to Lahaina, the capitol and favorite headquarters of the king.

Lele, as the Hawaiian village was known, was described by an initial European as the Venice of the Pacific because of the network of waterways and canals required to cultivate the taro food plant. Unlike many Pacific Islands over time, Maui has never suffered a food famine.

Hawaiians gradually embraced most things Western including the construction of the King's official buildings. The quality and craftsmanship with these new materials was often of questionable durability due to lack of experienced workmen. Nothing remains today.

As Maui became an agricultural outer island in the 1850's the new King Kamehameha IV moved the government to the deep-water port village of Honolulu.

Lahaina was a small backwater town until the completion of the Pali road tunnel in 1927 and the subsequent age of modern tourism arrived beginning in the 60's.

The always sunny dry climate on the protected south shore makes the picturesque Lahaina town a delight to visit.

Most of Maui visitors, if they are not already staying on the West Side, end up their sooner or later- and with good reason. The West Side is one of the most culturally and recreationally rich areas on the island.

With the colorful history of Lahaina, excitement of Ka'anapali, the quiet residential feel of Kahana and the fabulous beauty of Kapalua, the West Side has opportunities galore for all kinds vacation activities.

Lahaina's history is rich with chiefs and kings, captains and whales. The old whaling port's past is as colorful as the sea, the fields and the West Maui mountains surrounding the town.

Fierce battles for supremacy were fought near Lahaina. On the site now occupied by Ka'anapali's Hyatt and Marriott hotels, two brothers fought the battle of Koko O Na Moku, or Blood of the Islands, for Maui's throne after King Kekaulike died.

Captain James Cook, the European discoverer of Hawaii, sighted Maui in 1778, though indications are he never landed here. Twelve years later, Kamehameha the Great conquered Maui and later named Lahaina the capital of his kingdom.

Old Lahaina Towne bustled in the following century, particularly as growing numbers of whalers found it a perfect winter port. Midway between whaling grounds east of Japan and home in Nantucket, Lahaina became a favorite port for sailors to indulge in wine, women and song.

Whaling collapsed later in the century with the advent of crude oil refining. As whaling died, so did much of Lahaina. The capital moved to Honolulu,

Destination
LAHAINA

and except for the activity brought about by plantation life, Lahaina fell asleep.

The town began to reawaken 20 years ago when tourism started being developed in a big way. Lahaina's eyes are wide open again now as its streets teem with visitors from abroad who find the quaint town an ideal spot for a holiday.

For history, the Baldwin Home at Front and Dickenson Street is a good place to begin a tour. It was the mid-19th century home of missionary Dr. Dwight Baldwin and has been restored as a museum by the Lahaina Restoration Society.

Other Restoration Society projects worth visiting

are the Old Prison and the Wo Hing Temple. The popular picturesque sailing vessel, the Carthaginian, is berthed in Lahaina Harbor, with its own museum in its holds.

Shopping in old Lahaina town and plying the wharf for its recreational activities are also high on most visitors' list of things to do. Fine art galleries abound here, as do interesting shops and outstanding restaurants. A wealth of ocean boating activities are available at the wharf and there are ample opportunities in this town for nightlife fun. A look beyond the shops, into Lahaina's rich past, also can be a rewarding island diversion all by itself.

From high above, Lahaina's true beauty can be absorbed all at once. Photo by Ron Dahlquist.

Old Lahaina Town

HISTORICAL SITES

The blue numbered locations on this map refer to Lahaina's Historical Sites, which you can visit as you walk through Old Lahaina Town. For more information on each location, see "A Walk Through Lahaina's History" on the next two pages.

1 The Master's Reading Room
2 The Baldwin House
3 Richard's House
4 Taro Patch
5 The Hauola Stone
6 The Brick Palace
7 The Carthaginian
8 Pioneer Inn
9 The Banyan Tree
10 The Lahaina Courthouse
11 The Fort
12 Whaler's Canal
13 The Government Market
14 The Episcopal Church
15 Hale Piula
16 Maluuluolele Park
17 Waine'e Church
18 Waine'e Churchyard
19 Hongwanji Mission
20 David Malo's House
21 Hale Pa'ahao (Old Prison)
22 Episcopal Cemetery
23 Hale Aloha
24 Buddhist Church
25 Luakini Street
26 Maria Lanakila Church
27 Seamen's Cemetery
28 Hale Pa'i (House of Printing)
29 Wo Hing Temple
30 Seaman's Hospital
31 Buddha/Jodo Mission

DINING

A. Aloha Mixed Plate
B. BJ's Chicago Pizza
C. Cheeseburger In Paradise
D. Hecocks Oceanfront Dining
E. Kobe Japanese Steakhouse
F. Lahaina Cannery Mall
    • Compadre's Bar & Grill
    • Edo Japan Teppanyaki
G. Longhi's
O. Maui Princess
H. Maui Tacos
I. Pioneer Inn Restaurant
K. Woody's Oceanfront Grill

ACTIVITIES

D. Feast at Lele
L. Expeditions
M. The Hawaii Experience Dome Theater
F. Lahaina Cannery Mall
    • Klahani Travel
J. Maui Myth & Magic • "Ulalena"
N. Old Lahaina Luau

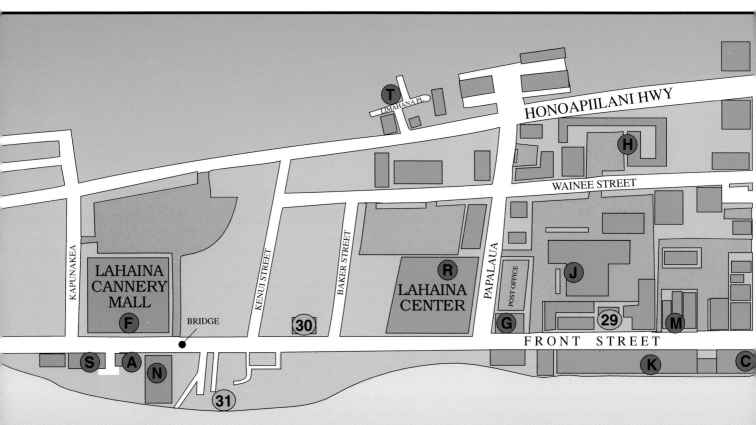

Walking Map

SHOPPING

Q. Dan's Greenhouse
K. Gary's Island Resort Wear
M. The Hawaii Experience Dome Theater
F. Lahaina Cannery Mall
- Groove 2 Music
- Lahaina Motorcycle Works
- Maui Dive Shop
- Maui Treasures
- Roland's Shoes
- Totally Hawaiian Gift Gallery
R. Lahaina Center
- Local Motion
U. Lahaina Galleries
S. Local Motion (across from Lahaina Cannery)
T. Lost World Arts
I. Pioneer Inn Shopping Center
U. Andrea Smith, Artist (Lahaina Galleries)

▬ PARKING

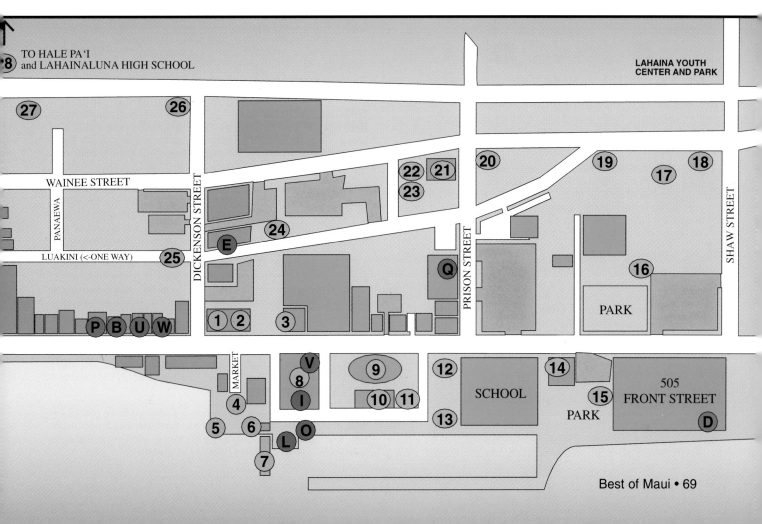

TO HALE PA'I and LAHAINALUNA HIGH SCHOOL

LAHAINA YOUTH CENTER AND PARK

WAINEE STREET

PANAEWA

LUAKINI (<-ONE WAY)

DICKENSON STREET

PRISON STREET

SHAW STREET

MARKET

SCHOOL

PARK

505 FRONT STREET

PARK

A WALK THROUGH LAHAINA'S HISTORY

Lahaina, the first capital of the Hawaiian Kingdom, is made for strolling. A seat of royal rule since the sixteenth century, most landmarks surviving today date from contact with European civilization. Refer to the Lahaina map on pages 20 and 21 for numbered locations of each historical site.

■ Existing Structures   ● Sites Only

1 THE MASTER'S READING ROOM • The Master's Reading Room coral block and field-stone construction has been preserved exactly as originally built in 1834. Once used as a storeroom for the missionaries, it was converted into an "officer's club" for the masters and officers of the whaling vessels replenishing their supplies in Lahaina. Visit for maps and printed information about Lahaina.

2 THE BALDWIN HOME • Shaded by kukui nut trees, the stone wall of the restored Baldwin Home, the oldest building on Maui, is an inviting spot to sit and watch the world go by. Docents offer a lively tour through the home of Dwight Baldwin, the frit medical missionary who served the Lahaina area from the mid-1830s to 1868. Open daily. Admission charge: $2

3 RICHARDS' HOUSE • William Richards was the first Protestant missionary to Lahaina, and the Richards' House was the first coral stone house in the islands, on the site of the present Campbell Park. Richards left the mission in the mid-1830s to work directly for the kingdom as chaplain, teacher and translator to Kamehameha III. He helped draw up the constitution, traveled to the United States and Europe as the king's envoy, seeking recognition of the kingdom's independence, and served as the Minister of Education. He eventually retired to New England where he died in 1847 and his body was returned for burial in the Waine'e Churchyard [18].

4 TARO PATCH • This spot, now the Lahaina Library, was part of the Old Lahaina system of many waterways, streams, ponds, and flooded taro patches. Ancient Hawaiians considered taro the "staff of life." Every part of the taro plant is edible: leaf, stem, and the underground corm.

5 THE HAUOLA STONE • This stone is popularly believed to have been used by the Hawaiians as a healing place.

6 THE "BRICK PALACE" • Built around the year 1800 by two ex-convicts from the British penal colony at Botany Bay, Australia, it was almost certainly the first western building in the islands. Constructed at the command of Kamehameha I, it was used intermittently as a storehouse and a residence until the 1850s. The cornerstones and foundations have been excavated and a display built by the Lahaina Restoration Foundation for the Maui County Historic Commission.

7 THE CARTHAGINIAN • Typical of the fast, small freighters that plied Hawaii's waters, the Carthaginian is a replica of a 19th century brig. An exhibit on whales and whaling, a superb film about humpbacks, and an original whale boat from Alaska are on display on board. Open daily 9am to 4:30pm. Admission: $2.

8 PIONEER INN • The clientele was rough when the Pioneer Inn first opened its doors in 1901. Posted in the lobby are the original hilarious house rules governing behavior. The only visitor accommodation in West Maui until the late 1950s, the Lahaina landmark was and remains a favorite of visiting sailors and adventurers from around the world.

9 THE BANYAN TREE • The coolest spot in Lahaina, the shady branches of the banyan from India cover more than two-thirds of an acre. Planted in April 1873 to mark the fiftieth anniversary of the beginning of the Protestant missionary work in Lahaina, the banyan is a popular setting for sidewalk art shows.

10 THE LAHAINA COURTHOUSE • A custom house, a post office, and a police court have all been housed in the building at various times in its history. Built after a big storm in 1858, the building now is home to the Lahaina Arts Society. Today jail cells in the basement contain works of art instead of prisoners.

11 THE FORT • Sailors visiting Lahaina objected to the missionary ban on native women visiting their ships. After they fired cannonballs into the town in protest, they were thrown into the fort that once stood here. The reconstructed remains of one wall still stands.

12 WHALER'S CANAL • Lahaina had not natural harbor like Honolulu's — one an open roadstead — and the whaler's small "chase boats" had to come in from the deep-water offshore anchorage to trade. In the early 1840s, the United States consular representative dug a canal to a basin near the market, and charged a fee for its use. After a few years, the government took over the canal and built a thatched market house with stalls, which almost immediately burned. The canal was filled in 1913.

13 GOVERNMENT MARKET • Here all trade between natives and ships was carried on. "These are the things which I strictly forbid," ran the edict of Princess Nahi'ena'ena in 1833, "overcharging, under-selling... wrangling, breaking of bargains, enticing, pursuing, chasing a boat, greediness... I hereby forbid women from going to the market enclosure for the purpose of sight-seeing or to stand idly by..." Despite this, the area around the market was noted for its gamy activities, and was called Rotten Row.

14 EPISCOPAL CHURCH • Founded in 1862, the present building dated from 1927, and is notable for an altar painting depicting a Hawaiian Madonna and colorful endemic plants and birds.

15 HALE PIULA • "Iron-reef house," a large two-story stone building with a surrounding piazza, was built in the late 1830s as a palace for Kamehameha III. It was not a success. In fact, it was never finished. The king preferred to sleep in a small thatch hut nearby. By the mid-1840s, the kind and his advisers were spending more time at Honolulu than Lahaina, and Hale Piula fell into disrepair. It was used as a courthouse for some time, and after a gale damaged it badly in 1858 its stones were used to build the present Courthouse [10].

16 MALUULUOLELE PARK • The bland, flat surface of Maluuluolele Park hides one of the most interesting parts of old Lahaina. Once there was a pond here, called Mokuhinia, home of a powerful water spirit in the form of a lizard or dragon. A tiny island in the pond, Mokuula, was for decades a home of Maui chiefs, and then a residence of three Kamehameha kings. Several important chiefs of the early 1800s were buried there. Kamehameha III used to receive visitors at the royal tomb in the late 1830s and early 1840s, showing them the large burial chamber, with its mirrors, velvet draperies, chairs and kahili (feathered staffs), and ornate coffins. Long after the chiefs' remains were removed, the pond was filled and the island leveled in 1918.

17 WAINE'E CHURCH • The first stone church in the islands, built between 1828 and 1832 by natives under the direction of their chiefs for the Protestant mission. It could seat 3,000 Hawaiians packed together on the floor. A whirlwind unroofed the church and blew down the belfry in 1858; the bell, once described as "none too sonorous," fell a hundred feet undamaged. In 1894, native royalists protesting the annex-ation of Hawaii by the U.S. burned the church. Rebuilt, it burned again in 1947, was rebuilt, and was demolished by another whirlwind in 1951. The new church, dedicated in 1953, was renamed Waiola, "Water of Life."

18 WAINE'E CHURCHYARD • Here lies history. Here are buried Hawaiian chiefs and commoners, seamen, missionaries (and missionaries' children, for infant mortality was sadly high). Here and there is a reminder of the old custom of marking the tomb with a glass-framed picture. Among the stones are those of Governor Hoapili and his wife Kalakua, and pioneer missionary William Richards [3].

19 HONGWANJI MISSION • Members of the Buddhist Hongwanji Mission have been meeting here since 1910, when they put up a small temple and a language school. The present building dates from 1927.

20 DAVID MALO'S HOUSE • Was located near the junction of Prison Road and Waine'e Street. Malo, educated at Lahainaluna Seminary as an adult, was the first renowned Hawaiian scholar and philosopher. He developed a keen sense of judgement and was a prime mover in framing the bill of rights and the constitution. His account of the ancient culture, *Hawaiian Antiquities*, has become a classic. Bitter about growing white control of Hawaii, he asked to be buried "above the tide of the foreign invasion" and his grave site is on the top of Mt. Ball, above the school. David Malo Day is celebrated annually at the high school in late spring.

21 HALE PA'AHAO • "Stuck-in-irons-house," was Lahaina's prison from the 1850s. Today the park-like, recently refurbished com-pound hosts community functions. This second prison in Lahaina's battle between vice and virtue had a more healthful design than the old fort it replaced.

22 EPISCOPAL CEMETERY • Located on Waine'e Street. Contains burial sites of many early families on Maui who joined the Anglican Church after the Archbishop of Canterbury in England was specifically requested to form a church in Hawai'i by Queen Emma.

23 HALE ALOHA • Viewable from the cemetary. The "House of Love" was built by native Protestants in "commemoration of God's causing Lahaina to escape the smallpox, while it desolated O'ahu in 1853, carrying off 5,000-6,000 of its population. Restored in 1974.

24 BUDDHIST CHURCH OF THE SHINGON SECT • The green paint and simple wooden architectural style is typical of church buildings put up all over Maui in the plantation area, when Japanese laborers were imported to work in the sugar fields.

25 LUAKINI STREET • Along Luakini Street in 1837 passed the funeral procession of the tragic Princess Nahi'ena'ena. Caught between the ancient and the modern world, she alternately worshipped the Protes-tant God, and yearned after the old traditions, in which a union with her brother, Kamehameha III, would have preserved the purity of the royal family. She had a son by the king in August, 1836. The boy lived only a few hours, and Nahi'enah'ena herself died in December. She was twenty-one. A path to her burial sight was made through stands of breadfruit and koa trees. It became known as Luakini Street, after the Hawaiian word for the sacrificial heiau, the state temples of the old religion.

26 MARIA LANAKILA CHURCH • Located on Dickenson Street near Waine'e Street. The first Roman Catholic mass was cel-ebrated on Maui in 1841, and there had been a Catholic church on this site since 1846. The present church, a concrete replica of an earlier wooden structure, dated from 1928.

27 SEAMEN'S CEMETERY • Located on Waine'e Street. Herman Melville's cousin was buried here, and one of Melville's shipmates as well, who died in the Seamen's Hospital [30] of a "disreputable disease.' Over the years, the marked graves of the sailors gradually disappeared, until now only one or two are identifiable.

28 HALE PA'I • The printing house of Lahainaluna Seminary, founded by Protestant missionaries in 1831, turned out hundreds of thousands of pages of material in the Hawaiian language. The school is the oldest educational institution west of the Rockies and now serves as the public high school for the Lahaina area. The printing shop was restored in 1980-82. An exhibit features a replica of the original Ramage press and facsimiles of early printing. Museum open Monday-Friday, 10am-3pm.

29 WO HING TEMPLE • A handsome restored Victorian house which formerly served as a clubhouse and fraternal organization for the Chinese of Lahaina. The Taoist temple room is upstairs.

30 SEAMAN'S HOSPITAL • Built in the 1830s as a party hideaway for the young Kamehameha III who liked to drink ardent spirit and gamble with the sailors. After he matured and spent more time in Honolulu the structure was a hospital for sailors recovering from the hazardous sea voyage. Reconstructed in the 70s, a human skeleton found under the northeast cornerstone is consistent with historical reports of a pre-western Hawaiian practice.

31 BUDDHA STATUE/JODO MISSION • The statue of Buddha at the Jodo Mission near Mala Wharf was erected to mark the hundredth anniversary of the arrival of the first Japanese plantation laborers in 1868. The grounds and building of the mission are open to the public.

Moku'ula
Birth of a Culture

by Karee Carlucci
Images courtesy Friends of Moku'ula

DID YOU KNOW that one of the most significant archaeological finds in the Hawaiian and Polynesian culture is sitting under a baseball field and parking lot in Lahaina? Moku'ula, Lahaina's "sacred island," was a royal residence for the Ali'i of Maui for centuries. This royal complex was situated in the middle of Loko O Mokuhinia, a natural pond spanning 14 acres, and well over a thousand years old.

Let's go back to the beginning . . . as the mists cloak Kahalawai (Hawaiian name for West Maui Mountains) and the life-giving rains descend from Mauna Ka Wahine and into Kaua'ula Valley (mountain and valley that rises above Moku'ula), the gods walked the earth. In the legend of the creation of Rapa Nui (Easter Island), a lizard-like god was born through Mauna Te Vahine (Mauna Ka Wahine) in a distant place called Tauraura (Kaua'ula). At birth, this lizard god leapt from the womb of the "mountain of the woman" and, with its umbilical cord still attached, flew south over the Pacific Ocean where its piko (umbilicus) detached and fell into the sea. The umbilicus became the island Te Piko O Te Fenua which means, "the umbilicus of the earth," the name given to Rapa Nui by its early inhabitants.

On Maui, the familial line of Pi'ilani (the highest royal family) was tied to the powerful Mo'o Akua (lizard-like god). At the death of the Pi'ilani high chiefess, the rite of deification was performed and she became the sacred lizard goddess known as Kihawahine. This goddess was the guardian for the royal Mokuhinia ponds and Moku'ula island. As water implies life and is considered sacred to the Hawaiians, it is always protected by the Mo'o Akua. Although Moku'ula is literally translated today as "sacred island," another translation is "mo'o ku'ula" (or shrine of the lizard god); likewise, Mokuhinia can be translated as "mo'o kuhiwnia" (or abundant lizard god).

The histories of two Polynesian cultures appear to have begun at Moku'ula. Because of this, in 1998, Moku'ula was recognized and honored by the Mayor of Rapa Nui in a ceremony to establish a "sister island" relationship between Rapa Nui and Maui, which took place at Moku'ula in Lahaina.

In Hawaiian history, Moku'ula has played a major role as the center of rule for its kingdom. King Kamehameha I and his successor sons all resided there, and Moku'ula emerged as a focus (or piko) for native Hawaiian religion and statecraft. After the battle of 'Iao Valley in 1790 which resulted in unifying the Hawaiian Islands, King Kamehameha the Great made a political move to unite himself with the women of Maui's royal line. Their children would then be legitimate heirs to Hawai'i, Maui, Moloka'i and Lana'i, as well as O'ahu.

Shortly after the death of Kamehameha the Great in 1819, the first Christian missionaries arrived in Lahaina. Kamehameha's first wife, the sacred Queen Keopuolani, became an early convert. But in the following years, while new Christian churches were being erected, slowly eradicating Hawaiian heiau temples, Lahaina's sacred island of Moku'ula remained as a spiritual sanctuary.

Kamehameha III succeeded to the throne as a child, after the death of his older brother in 1825. He was left under the care of Regent Ka'ahumanu (Kamehameha the Great's second wife) and the Maui Governor, who were devout Christians. As the young king grew older, he became increasingly restless with the teachings of the Protestant missionaries in Lahaina, and challenged his guardians. He maintained the island as an umbilicus for the Hawaiian kingdom and the old kapu system of proprietary restrictions.

When the king's wife died in childbirth along with their first child, Kamehameha III prepared for the funeral by building a large stone tomb at Moku'ula. In addition, he had the royal remains of his sacred mother and other chiefs brought to this new mausoleum. From 1837 to 1845, Moku'ula would be King Kamehameha III's home and the kingdom's symbol.

During this period of great change in the Hawaiian kingdom, Moku'ula became a source of security and privacy for the royal family. The island was connected to Front Street by a gated causeway guarded by sentries. There was a pier on the opposite side from which canoes could be launched. Kamehameha III would see chosen visitors and entertain special guests on the island; he and his new wife spent much of their time in cool pili grass houses or under hau tree bowers in the compound.

The Royal Court left Lahaina in 1845, when it was clear that the focus of power, trade and finance was shifting to Honolulu. Moku'ula was still visited by royalty for many years, but the freshwater Mokuhinia pond was shrinking and its water was becoming stagnant. The demands of the sugarcane plantations had diverted much of the water which had formerly fed the fishponds.

In 1913 a group of businessmen, including the heads of Pioneer Mill and the Pioneer Hotel, started a public project which filled in Mokuhinia Pond with coral rubble dredged from Lahaina Harbor. By Executive Order of the Territory of Hawaii in 1918, the newly-filled pond was turned over to the County of Maui for use as the park you see today.

The first archaeological excavations in 1993 uncovered the remains of the island's pier, retaining wall and a holding pond. The royal palace site in Lahaina was found 2-3 feet below the surface of the County baseball park, near the intersection of Front and Shaw Streets. Now, Moku'ula is seen as an island of continuity. Nearly forgotten for 80 years, it is being recaptured in the imaginations and dedication of a new generation of Hawaiians.

Friends of Moku'ula, Inc. was established in 1995 to preserve and ultimately restore the island and ponds, as well as create an interactive site where visitors and residents can experience cultural traditions and learn the history of pre-contact Hawai'i. Lahaina remains the bridge to Maui's past, and the heart of Lahaina continues to pulse at Moku'ula, the spiritual center of the Hawaiian Kingdom.

I Ka Wa Mamua, Ka Wa Mahope
"The Future is in the Past."

Ka'anapali Beach area before the arrival of the Europeans. Along the beach were canoe houses, dwelling compounds and all the activities of fishing and transportation. Two hundred years later this area is a billion-dollar destination resort. Painting courtesy of Herb Kane, collection of AMFAC, Inc.

Just a few miles up the road from Lahaina is a beautiful pristine beach and the first destination resort on Maui...Ka'anapali. The Ka'anapali Resort includes many fabulous resort hotels and condominiums fronting Ka'anapali Beach, a magnificent stretch of white sand. In Ka'anapali you'll find casual to elegant restaurants, rooms from modest to luxury prices, just about every kind of beach activity there is, some fantastic snorkeling at famous Black Rock and at Whaler's Village, Maui's most successful shopping center, a whale museum.

The hotels along this stretch of beach also provide lots of outstanding restaurants, glittering night spots and exciting events and concerts throughout the year including a Hawaiian cultural festival, Na Mele O Maui, a keiki (child) hula festival and a Hawaiian Cultural Arts Expo.

Black Rock, or Pu'u Keka'a, was once a sacred location to the ancient Hawaiians. They revered it as a place where the spirits of the dead went to leap from this world to the next. It was considered extremely brave to leap from the same spot as the spirits of the dead. This leap is recreated

each evening at sunset by a diver from the Sheraton Maui, and during the day by daring tourist.

Black Rock, along with many other sites in Ka'anapali, becomes even more fascinating than usual when you learn about the mythology and history behind it. This fascination may help explain why a great majority of visitors to Maui stay in Ka'anapali.

The Ka'anapali Resort is located on Maui's western shore, just five minutes away from Kapalua/West Maui Airport. The picturesque drive from Maui's main airport, located in Kahalui, takes the visitor along Maui's beautiful coast and is about 23 miles and roughly 40 minutes away from Ka'anapali.

The hotels and condominiums of Ka'anapali are some of the best in the world and cater to their guests every whim. In the center of the resort lies the green expanse of the Ka'anapali Golf Courses. The North and South courses offer an unforgettable experience for any avid golfer and the North Course host the Ka'anapali Classic Senior PGA Tour tournament in October. Tennis is another sport per-

Destination
KAANAPALI

fectly suited to the Ka'anapali Resort. There are many courts available for play and most of them are lighted to allow play after sunset.

For the historically minded, the Whalers Village 'Whale Museum of the Pacific' is a fascinating look at a period of Maui's history. The museum, which is believed to have the largest collection of whaling memorabilia in the world, has just been expanded to include 'Hale Kohala'.

Another reminder of Maui's simpler times can not only be seen, but ridden! The Lahaina Ka'anapali and Pacific Railroad, known more simply as the Sugar Cane Train, travels between Lahaina and Ka'anapali on its rails that were built during the boom of the great sugar industry. The train once helped move the harvested sugar from fields of Ka'anapali to Pioneer Mill in Lahaina and from there to the harbors to be loaded onto the cargo ships. Now it serves the needs of the tourism industry by providing a scenic ride and nostalgic trip back in time. The Sugar Cane Train is a must for every visitor on Maui.

Another way to enjoy the way it used to be in Lahaina is to ride in a 1929 Model A Ford Phaelin with Classy Taxi for the same rates as a regular taxi.

Once you've seen everything on land, it's time to hit the beach for ocean activities. Snorkeling should be one of the activities you choose, because Ka'anapali's reefs provides some of the most colorful underwater spectacles to be seen anywhere. The area around Black Rock is an exceptional place to start. The water is shallow, and the reefs are populated with exotic sea creatures that are used to the presence of people.

From November to May, whale watching fever strikes the island when the great humpback whales frolic in the waters off of Ka'a napali. For visitors that would like a closer look at the humpbacks than from the beach, the hotel lanai, or an ocean side restaurant there are whale watch cruises available and can be booked right in the hotel.

The humpback whale is an endangered animal and is protected by international law. They migrate to Hawaii's waters in the winter to breed and bear their young. During the summer, they feed on plankton off the Alaskan coast.

Ka'anapali, Hawaii's first destination resort, houses six luxury hotels and is built on four miles of glorious beach. Photo by Randy Hufford.

KA'ANAPALI

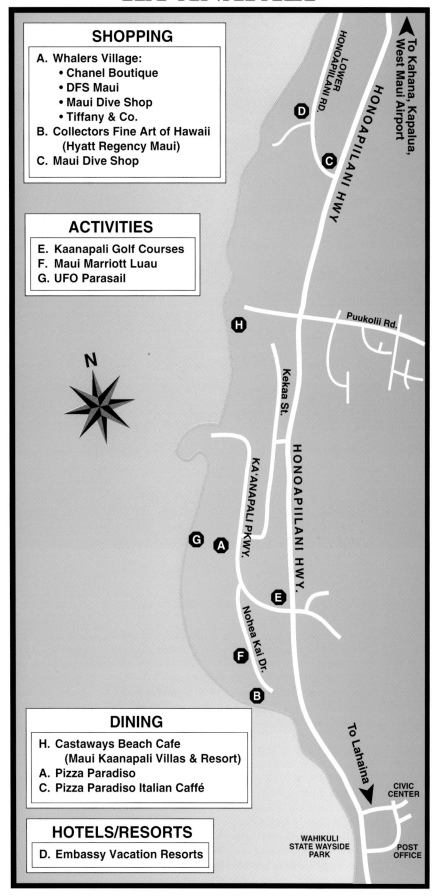

SHOPPING

A. Whalers Village:
  • Chanel Boutique
  • DFS Maui
  • Maui Dive Shop
  • Tiffany & Co.
B. Collectors Fine Art of Hawaii
   (Hyatt Regency Maui)
C. Maui Dive Shop

ACTIVITIES

E. Kaanapali Golf Courses
F. Maui Marriott Luau
G. UFO Parasail

DINING

H. Castaways Beach Cafe
   (Maui Kaanapali Villas & Resort)
A. Pizza Paradiso
C. Pizza Paradiso Italian Caffé

HOTELS/RESORTS

D. Embassy Vacation Resorts

Whether you're driving along the coast, lying on the beach or enjoying a cocktail on your lanai during whale watching season it's best to keep your eyes toward the ocean.

If Kaanapali's charms prove to be irresistibly attractive, don't forget that you could be calling Kaanapali your second home by purchasing a homesite. Kaanapali's developer, Amfac/JMB Hawaii, Inc. has developed Kaanapali's first gated residential community, Kaanapali Golf Estates. This subdivision is adjacent to the Kaanapali Golf Courses and has a spectacular view of the resort, the Pacific Ocean, Lanai and Molokai.

Whatever your tropical island pleasure, you are bound to find it here along the Kaanapali coastline. Kaanapali is where the world comes to play!

For a listing of annual events in the Kaanapali area see the Maui Calendar of Events in the back of this book.

KA'ANAPALI LUAU & DINING DIRECTORY

MAUI MARRIOTT LUAU
Maui Marriott Hotel, Kaanapali Beach
(808) 661-LUAU (661-5828)
The Marriott Luau is renowned for its sumptuous feast and spectacular entertainment on breathtaking Kaanapali Beach. Each guest is greeted and adorned with a traditional shell lei. After a demonstration of island games and cultural activities, the imu ceremony begins. A kalua pig is dug out and prepared in the underground oven where it has spent hours roasting to perfection. The buffet showcases chicken Polynesian, broiled teriyaki beef steak, Island fish, lomi lomi salmon, fresh salads, poi (of course), unique desserts, and much more. Don't forget an exotic mai tai from the open bar. Dinner is followed by a Polynesian odyssey of song, dance and historic chants performed by a troupe of brightly-costumed entertainers. The evening reaches its peak with the spectacular Triple Fireknife performance. No visit to the Hawaiian Islands is complete without the experience of an authentic luau, and the Marriott Luau is one that you'll savor and remember for a long time afterward. Map to left; ad on next page.

CASTAWAY BEACH CAFE
Maui Kaanapali Villas & Resort, Kaanapali
(808) 661-9091
See page 32 for directory listing.

PIZZA PARADISO EXPRESS
Whalers Village, Kaanapali
(808) 667-0333
See page 38 for directory listing.

The Island's Hottest Show...

maui marriott LUAU

MAUI'S ONLY TRIPLE FIRE KNIFE ATTRACTION!

"MY FAMILY AND I KEEP COMING BACK, BACK & BACK EVERY YEAR!"
~ Chris Berman
T.V. Sports Announcer

VOTED BEST LUAU!
~ *San Francisco Chronicle*

CALL FOR SEASONAL DISCOUNTS FROM 10%-40% OFF.

Now is three times Hotter!

"WHENEVER FAMILY OR FRIENDS COME TO VISIT, WE ALWAYS MAKE SURE TO TREAT THEM TO THE HOTTEST SHOW IN TOWN... THE MARRIOTT LUAU."
~ *Pastor Akima, Harvest Chapel, Maui*

ALSO SEEN ON NBC® TODAY SHOW

Call the Luau Hotline: 661-LUAU (5828)
D.S.

ASK US ABOUT OUR GROUP DISCOUNTS, PRIVATE SHOWS, AARP SAVINGS, SHOW ONLY AND "SAME DAY BOOKING" DISCOUNTS.

Destination
NAPILI

Napili Bay is an ideal beach for beginners or families with small children, since its calm waters provide a safe and beautiful playground. Photo by Tony Novak-Clifford.

N apili, gateway to Kapalua, is located just 9 miles north of Lahaina. Napili has a lot to offer. When you arrive in Napili on the main highway you'll find Napili Plaza, which is host to a diverse selection of shops, restaurants and services. Napili Plaza also offers a crafts fair every Wednesday and Saturday from 10am to 4pm. Be sure to drop in and experience this unique plaza.

If you are looking for a great beach for snorkeling, scuba diving, or just basking in the sun, Napili Bay is for you. Napili Bay is protected from big waves most of the year. The water is calmer for safe activities — perfect for children and those unfamiliar with the ocean. The U-shaped Napili Bay offers rock and reef viewing and is abundant with sea life. This beach is known to be frequented by skim boarders — the steep start to the beach makes for excellent take-off into the surf. The Napili coastline also has some excellent surf spots. The surf is usually larger in the winter.

Napili is also popular with walking and jogging enthusiasts. This is the place to start a great walking experience into Kapalua. You can start near the lower road or the highway and walk the Napili-Kapalua loop. On your walk you will find beautiful luxury homes, plant life and flowers, large Norfolk pines, golf holes, etc... most of the loop even offers sidewalks.

═NAPILI ⊞ PLAZA

Visitors and locals alike enjoy the convenience of shopping and dining at Napili Plaza. Located nine miles north of Lahaina just before Kapalua Resort.

OTHER FINE SHOPS AND RESTAURANTS
- All Star Video ▪ Awesome Tees ▪
- Boss Frog's Surf and Dive Shop ▪ First Hawaiian Bank ▪
- Key To Life Chiropractor ▪ Mail Services Plus ▪
- Mama's Ribs & Rotisserie ▪ Napili Market ▪
- Napili Art Cetera Gallery ▪ Sakamoto Properties ▪
- Stanfield's West Maui Floral ▪ Subway ▪
- Valley Isle Dry Cleaners ▪

Management Office at (808) 877-3369, ext. 27 or 665-0546.
Craft Fair every Wed. & Sat., 10am-4pm.
Sponsored by the Hawaii Arthritis Foundation.

MAUI TACOS

Burritos! Nachos! Salsa Bar!
Featuring pineapple/lime marinated char-broiled steak and chicken, and island fish.

It's Mexican Food with Mauitude.™

Nothing over $6.95
Lahaina • Napili
Kihei • Kaahumanu

665-0222

www.mauitacos.com
See page 38 for details.

VOTED **BEST** COFFEE STORE
ON MAUI FOR **6 YEARS**

Kaahumanu Center
Kahului
871-6860

Napili Plaza
Napili-West Maui
669-4170

THE • COFFEE • STORE

Azeka Place
Kihei
875-4244

Maalaea Triangle
Maalaea
242-2779

Where we do a lot more than just coffee.

HIGHEST GRADES OF 100% KONA COFFEE and other coffees, teas, and gifts from Hawaii and around the world. The Best Cappuccino on Maui for those who like it hot, or our famous (secret recipe) Ice Blended Mocha for those who like it cold. Need to calm down or perk up, send e-mails, buy a gift, have a dessert, a light meal or a full lunch — come to The Coffee Store nearest you! Whether on Maui or back home — visit us at **www.mauicoffee.com**.
See page 32 for details.

ROXANA'S
Hair Affair

We are a full service beauty salon with a very professional staff.
Great Cuts ▪ Styling ▪ Color Technicians
Nails ▪ Gentle Perming ▪ Wedding Styles
large selection of professional products.
See page 50 for details. **669-7743**

Destination KAPALUA

Kapalua — 1,650 acres of quiet elegance. Photo by Ray Mains.

*J*ust 10 miles north of Lahaina is the historic community of Kapalua. Located amidst the only working pineapple plantation on Maui today, adjacent to the resort you can view the planting, growing and harvesting of this tropical fruit. In the late 1800s, Kapalua was part of Honolua Ranch, complete with Hereford herds, taro patches and fields of red coffee bean bushes. During the first half of this century, the plantation manager, H.P. Baldwin began the transition to pineapple along with various experimental agricultural efforts such as aloe, mango, and avocado. Hardwoods, eucalyptus and ironwood trees were also planted to conserve water and prevent soil erosion. Today, the 100-year old Cook pines that stand sentinel over the historic buildings and landmarks hint at the far-reaching planning that went into the beginnings of Kapalua.

With three white sand beaches, Kapalua invites watersports galore. Kapalua Bay, "America's Best Beach," is well-protected and has equipment available at the conveniently located Beach Activity desk. Oneloa Bay fronts a secluded stretch of beach adjacent to The Bay Course 5th hole. Honokahua Bay is the site of D.T. Fleming Park that is a favorite with Maui families and in waters north of Kapalua are the Marine Life Conservation Districts of Honolua and Mokule'ia Bays, teeming with tropical fish and sea turtles.

KAHANA to KAPALUA

SERVICES

B. **NAPILI PLAZA:**
- Roxana's Hair Affair

SHOPPING

C. **KAPALUA SHOPS:**
- Kapalua Logo Shops
- La Perle
- Lahaina Galleries (Andrea Smith)
- Hawaiian Quilt Collection

A. **KAHANA GATEWAY:**
- Maui Dive Shop

ACTIVITIES

D. Ironwood Ranch
E. Volcano Air Tours
G. Kapalua Golf Academy

DINING

F. China Boat
C. **KAPALUA SHOPS:**
- Maui Coffee Co.
- Sansei Restaurant & Sushi Bar

B. **NAPILI PLAZA:**
- Maui Tacos
- The Coffee Store

Kapalua is nature's perfect setting. Since its inception, the resort has preserved its unique blend of natural resources and scenic wonders through a variety of programs. One such program is the dedication of an 8,661-acre native rainforest to The Nature Conservancy of Hawaii to protect the indigenous flora and fauna in perpetuity.

Additionally, Kapalua's three Golf Courses have been established as Certified Audubon Cooperative Sanctuaries by the Audubon International. The courses were awarded this designation after meeting stringent environmental standards set forth by the Audubon International for water conservation, habitat enhancement, integrated pest management and more.

ACCENTS
Sundries & gifts. 669-5283

ELIZABETH DOYLE GALLERY
Studio art glass gallery. 665-0916

**HAIMOFF & HAIMOFF
CREATIONS IN GOLD**
Contemporary fine jewelry classics and original designs. 669-5213

JOURABCHI
International designer wear. 665-0000

KAPALUA BODY & BATH
Botanicals, lotions, aromatherapy and spa products for mind, body & spirit. 669-4059

KAPALUA DESIGNS
Specialty logo accessories & private label gifts. 669-1390

KAPALUA DISCOVERY CENTER
Learn about the island's environment, culture, history and the arts.

KAPALUA KIDS
Logo apparel & gifts for children. 669-0033

KAPALUA REALTY
Exclusive resort listings. 669-0210

LA PERLE
See facing page advertisement. 669-8466

LAHAINA GALLERIES
Fine art & sculpture. 669-0202

MANDALAY
Designer silks & cottons. 669-6170

MAUI COFFEE COMPANY
Espresso, Kona coffee and light fare. 669-9667

MCINERNY
Upscale designer fashions. 669-5266

REYN'S
Classic resort wear & accessories. 669-5260

SANSEI SEAFOOD RESTAURANT
Maui's most creative sushi and seafood. 669-6286

SOUTH SEAS
Exotic works of art from the Orient & South Seas. 669-1249

SPIRIT OF POLYNESIAN ART
Authentic Hawaiian Handicrafts. 669-2949

TROPICANA
Fine leather goods and European collections. 669-6649

Kapalua Shops

Twenty distinctive boutiques and galleries with trinkets and treasures from around the globe.

- Sculpture & Artifacts • Art Galleries
- Designer Fashions & Resortwear
- Fine Jewelry • Giftware & Sundries

Complimentary Hawaiian Entertainment is offered throughout the week

Tuesdays 10 a.m.
Slack Key Guitar

Thursdays 10 a.m.
Traditional Hula Show

Fridays 11:30 a.m.
Musical Aloha Presentation

Located adjacent to the Kapalua Bay Hotel
Ample free parking

THE KAPALUA LOGO SHOP

Home of the Kapalua Butterfly. The distinctive Kapalua logo adorns a fine array of fashions and accessories for family and friends. Perfect for vacation, work and home. 669-4172

LA PERLE

Offering a fabulous collection for exotic natural-color pearl jewelry that connoisseurs should not miss. **La Perle**, in French, is an expression meaning "The Gem". The most sought after gem now is the Tahitian Black Natural-Color Pearl. Wise shoppers should visit **La Perle** before choosing their "Perle Noire". 669-8466

HAWAIIAN QUILT COLLECTION

Beautiful hand-made Hawaiian quilts, pillows, wall hangings, kits and much more. We pamper those who are "Hawaiian at Heart". Check us out on the web at www.Hawaiian-Quilts.com. Tell us at which hotel you saw this ad in and receive a 15% discount on minimum $50 purchase. 665-1111

THE NEW KAPALUA GOLF ACADEMY AND VILLAGE COURSE CLUBHOUSE

Kapalua's metamorphosis continues with a $15 million development encompassing a state-of-the-art Kapalua Golf Academy and a new Village Course Clubhouse.

Located at the entry of the Kapalua resort, the Kapalua Golf Academy and practice facility designed by Hale Irwin, Kapalua's Senior PGA TOUR Touring Professional, offers a unique state-of-the-art golf facility unmatched in Hawaii. The new project features 85,000 sq. ft. of grass teeing area, several practice putting greens, greenside and fairway bunkers, an 18-hole putting course, minimum of eight target greens and specialty short game area.

The Kapalua Golf Academy utilizes the spacious practice areas for group and individual teaching and, in addition, features an approx. 3,500-square foot facility to house classroom instruction, video taping and physical training. Kapalua's staff of over 25 PGA Golf Professionals, the largest in the state, offers a wide variety of instruction. Programs will utilize indoor/outdoor "instruction bays'; computerized video for swing and putting analyzis; teeing area with practice/learning stations for all-weather instruction; as well as private lessons and daily clinics.

Additionally, the Academy features a three-day comprehensive Golf School that benefits players of all skill levels. This extensive training addresses putting, chipping, and bunker play, full swing digital video analysis and on-course instruction. A two-day "Player's School" is designed for the more experienced player — 12 handicap or less. Instruction focuses on reading greens and shot selection, specialty and scoring shots, practice management, psychology of playing, as well as a complete digital video analysis. A half-day school is also available as well as special rates for junior golfers.

All three Kapalua properties, The Ritz-Carlton, Kapalua, the Kapalua Bay Hotel and The Kapalua Villas, feature two or three-day Golf Academy packages.

Part of Kapalua's project will also include a new 27,000-square foot Village Course Clubhouse, which replaces the existing clubhouse. The new facility will feature Kapalua's largest golf retail shop, restaurant, a multi-purpose conference room, and a resort communication and computer hub. The design concept will be reminiscent of the plantation era with art and interior design complimenting Kapalua's past history. The clubhouse is slated for completion in May 2000.

"With three diverse golf courses and a learning center such as this, there will be few resorts that can match Kapalua's golf presentation and amenities," said Hale Irwin.

For more information, write or call The Kapalua Golf Academy, 1000 Office Road, Kapalua, Hawaii 96761; (808) 669-6500; info@kapaluagolfacademy.com.

The #1 Golf Resort in Hawaii...

...Just Got Better.
Introducing the Kapalua Golf Academy.

Opening in March 2000, the new state-of-the-art Kapalua Golf Academy is a full-service practice and instruction facility like no other in Hawaii. Designed by Kapalua's Touring Professional, Hale Irwin, it features:
- 85,000 square feet of grass teeing area
- 3,500 square foot learning center
- Practice bunkers, greens and fairways
- 18-hole putting course
- Indoor/outdoor instruction bays
- Half-, two- and three-day golf schools
- Private instruction

In addition, Kapalua is home to three championship courses – The Plantation, site of the PGA TOUR Mercedes Championships each January, The Bay and The Village.

For information on the Kapalua Golf Academy or any of Kapalua's award-winning courses, call toll-free 877-KAPALUA.

Kapalua
Maui

www.kapaluagolfacademy.com

THE KAPALUA GOLFING EXPERIENCE

Internationally known for superb golf, Kapalua offers championship play on one of its two Arnold Palmer-designed courses, The Bay and The Village, or The Plantation, a Coore & Crenshaw designed course. Golf Digest has named Kapalua's courses as "Three of Hawaii's Top Six." Additional accolades come from Golf Magazine who named Kapalua as one of 12 "Gold Medal Golf Resorts in America" for the seventh consecutive time.

Kapalua Bay Course has lured golfers from all corners of the globe since 1975. Sun-drenched beaches, tropical terrain and volcanic promontories enhance the beautiful and challenging 18 holes. Particularly distracting, the 357-yard par-four 4th hole is perched on a black lava peninsula framed by the blue Pacific.

Kapalua Village Course was opened in 1981 and climbs from the foot of the West Maui mountains to mingle with pineapple fields and Cook pines, ultimately to reach a beautiful, unsuspected lake. The panorama from the 7th tee encompasses Molokai and Lanai as well as much of West Maui in a sweep of natural beauty.

In January 1999, Kapalua broke ground on a state-of-the-art Golf Academy and new Village Course Clubhouse which will be located at the entry of the Kapalua resort. The Golf Academy and practice facility were designed by Hale Irwin, Kapalua's Senior PGA TOUR Touring Professional and U.S. Open Champion, and features multiple tee areas, putting greens and bunkers for a variety of practice conditions. In addition, a 3,500 square foot facility will house classroom instruction, video taping and physical training.

Opened in 1991, Kapalua Plantation Course melds with the native Hawaiian topography to form one of Hawaii's most dramatic golfing landscapes. On this 7,263-yard links-style course, golfers play in a pristine and expansive environment with low-lying vegetation offset by very large-scale terrain features, including massive bunkers and deep valleys. The Plantation Course is Kapalua's ultimate golf challenge and home of the annual PGA TOUR's Mercedes Championships, held each January.

A staff of PGA professionals work to complement Kapalua's golf experience by offering private instruction, one-day golf schools, video instruction and daily golf clinics. The three pro-shops are completely stocked with a variety of golf merchandise and accessories; most adorned with the famous butterfly logo.

Hale Irwin sums up the feeling pros and amateurs share at Kapalua. "There is something distinctly different about playing at Kapalua. Some days, I think it is the setting. Other days, I know it is the play. No matter what, it is an experience I always remember as only happening here. It is an experience that makes me feel this is home."

WEST MAUI MOUNTAIN HIKES

Above Kapalua, towering over the manicured golf courses and vast pineapple plantation, are the hauntingly beautiful West Maui Mountains, crowned with rainbows and streaming with waterfalls. In protected wilderness areas, some of the last stands of Hawaii's endemic flora continue to flourish and rare birds continue to sing in the trees.

The Kapalua Nature Society offers an exclusive hike into portions of the majestic West Maui Mountains. The Maunalei Arboretum Nature Walk is about 2 miles. Hike guides lead participants on a historical journey through nearly a century of plantation management activities including pineapple; cattle ranching; coffee production and a 70-year old arboretum.

LODGING

Kapalua is a community as well as a resort, with golf, tennis, dining, shopping, a grocery store and churches for full-time residents and visitors alike. The accommodations are world-class and offer something to suit every

Ironwood Ranch

Nestled high in Northwest Maui foothills, see the sunset on horseback or enjoy a picnic ride. All levels welcome. Call direct for more information or for a reservation.

日本人のお客様を歓迎いたします。

(808) 669-4991

FAST FACTS
Hrs: Mon-Sat
Phone: 669-4991
See Map page 33.

PHOTO COURTESY OF KAPALUA RESORT

lifestyle. The Kapalua Villas, managed by the Kapalua Land Company, is comprised of select condominium villas and luxury homes located throughout the resort. These vacation rentals provide guests with the space and privacy of a home in a resort setting.

The stunning oceanfront Ritz-Carlton, Kapalua offers island hospitality with sophisticated style. The hotel's two six-story wings are contoured along the rolling Bay Course terrain and sited to take advantage of the surrounding panorama of ocean, mountain and fairways.

Kapalua Bay Hotel, managed by Starwood Hotels & Resorts under The Luxury Collection brand, is a charming hotel situated above Kapalua Bay that features a spectacular 30-foot ceiling in the lobby that affords a panoramic view from the strolling gardens to the ocean and neighbor islands beyond.

TENNIS TIME

Known as one of America's premier tennis destinations, Kapalua's Tennis Club has consistently been honored by Tennis Magazine as one of the "50 Greatest US Tennis Resorts."

Play in the garden or by the sea at two full-service tennis facilities, The Tennis Garden and The Village Tennis Center. Each facility features 10 plexi-pave courts (8 lighted), full-service pro-shops, snack bars, lounge areas and teaching pros. Offered daily are "Hit with the Pro" sessions and special "Stroke of the Day" clinics. For those seeking a more concentrated lesson, 3 or 5 day tennis camps are available from June to December. Individual or group instruction, including use of video equipment,

matchmaking services, NRTP Rating Sessions and Pro Drills are also available.

UNIQUE GIFTS IN UNIQUE SHOPS

The Kapalua Shops are an eclectic grouping of boutiques and galleries presenting a truly unique merchandise selection. With over twenty distinctly different stores, shoppers are sure to find something special. Located just above Kapalua Bay, The Shops offer a relaxed open air courtyard which encourages leisurely browsing among the fascinating trinkets and treasures. Here at The Shops you'll also find the home of the famous Kapalua butterfly logo with an array of logo "goodies" available at Kapalua Logo Shop, Kapalua Kids, Kapalua Designs and Kapalua Body & Bath. Complimentary Hawaiian Entertainment is held on Tuesdays at 10am, Thursdays at 10am, and Fridays at 11am.

KAPALUA DISCOVERY CENTER

Kapalua's Discovery Center, located in The Kapalua Shops, provides a one-of-a-kind experience for visitors to learn about the island's environment, culture and history. The Center features exhibits of Hawaii's endangered species; information on the company's Pu'u Kukui Preserve rainforest; displays of ancient Hawaiian artifacts and native Hawaiian plants.

LIVING AT KAPALUA

With four multi-family neighborhoods and three single-family communities, Kapalua offers residential living opportunities to suit every lifestyle. Homes,

The annual PGA TOUR Mercedes Championships is held each January at Kapalua's Plantation Course.

The Signature Hole (#5) at Kapalua's Bay Course.

homesites and condominium units are all located with the heart of this 1,650-acre master-planned resort, providing access to the multitude of amenities that are available to residents.

For those seeking to make Kapalua home, Kapalua Realty's on-site sales office is staffed with agents who specialize in Kapalua properties, earning them the distinction as "The Official Kapalua Experts." The sales office is located at the Kapalua Shops and is open 365 days a year.

THE ART SCHOOL AT KAPALUA

In addition to a resort-wide collection of fine local and national artwork and crafts in public spaces, The Art School at Kapalua provides an educational opportunity to residents and visitors. Staffed by art professionals, this not-for-profit facility features a year-round program of classes, workshops and exhibits. Walk-ins are welcome.

DINING AT KAPALUA

Long known for the reputation of its exceptional restaurants, Kapalua offers twelve diverse dining options from casual to elegant at The Ritz-Carlton, Kapalua, Kapalua Bay Hotel, The Bay Club, Jameson's Grill & Bar, Plantation House, The Village Cafe and Sansei Restaurant & Sushi Bar. Each restaurant is unique in its decor and bill-of-fare with Continental, Euro-Asian, Mediterranean, Pacific Rim, Hawaiian, Japanese and just plain "American" cuisines represented.

Sansei Restaurant & Sushi Bar, Maui's most creative sushi and seafood, has something for everyone. They specialize in the freshest fish available, along with Pacific Rim and other specialties, all at reasonable prices.

SPECIAL EVENTS

Kapalua is home to some of the most famous and spectacular events held annually, including the PGA TOUR Mercedes Championships, and the Kapalua

Wine and Food Symposium. For a complete listing of Kapalua Special Events, see the Calendar on page 128.

PINEAPPLE PLANTATION TOURS

Hawaii's king of fruits is the subject of Maui's onlyHawaiian Pineapple Plantation Tours offered by Maui Pineapple Company, Ltd. With the breathtaking views along the slopes of the West Maui Mountains, the public can tour the plantation of Hawaii's largest and only pineapple canner.

Led by long-time plantation workers, colorful commentary weaves the history of the area with current facts on ananas (pineapple) in these special 2 $^1/_2$ hour tours. Participants will ride to fields being harvested that very day, learn first-hand about the unique growing and harvesting cycle of Hawaii's "king of fruits," and view some of Maui's most spectacular scenery. As a momento of their tour, visitors will have the opportunity to pick their own pineapple to take home — an authentic plantation experience.

Two tours are offered Mondays through Fridays, 9:30am-12noon and 1:00pm-3:30pm. Cost is $26 per person and includes a pineapple to take home. Minimum age is 12 years to participate.

Reservations are recommended; participants check-in at the Kapalua Resort Activity Desk located in The Kapalua Villas, across from the Honolua Store.

KAPALUA-WEST MAUI AIRPORT

Only a few air carriers are allowed to use this airport. Maui Air & Volcano Air Tours take passengers on multi-island tours from Kapalua, including to the active volcano area on the Big Island of Hawaii, as well as private charters for guest who prefer their own custom tour and travel.

HORSEBACK RIDING

The Ironwood Ranch is nestled high in the foothills of northwest Maui. They offer horseback rides through remote, tranquil tropical areas. Trails offer panoramic ocean views to neighboring Molokai and Lanai. Riders are privy to explore terrain only accessible by horseback: the island's largest pineapple plantation, secluded mountain valleys and a bamboo forest.

Visitors can choose from a host of rides and times to accommodate ability and vacation schedules. Each ride is unique — varying from a three-hour morning picnic ride complete with a hike — to a late afternoon sunset ride. All rides are walking-paced except for the Ironwood Odyssey, designed for advanced riders.

The new horseback activity is located on restricted farmlands and transportation is provided to and from the ranch from West Maui resorts. Specializing in small, personalized groups, riders are matched to horses by their ability; all rides are guided. Ironwood Ranch offers these exclusive trail rides Monday through Saturday.

Destination
LANAI

Miles of uninhabited beaches line Lanai's northern coast. Photo by Ron Dahlquist.

Lanai is perhaps the least known, and least visited, of all the Hawaiian Islands. Even the ancient Polynesian settlers of the Hawaiian Islands did not settle Lanai until 500 years after they had settled the other islands. Why the Polynesians ignored Lanai is unknown. It is known, however, why tourists largely ignore Lanai today. Lanai's econ-omy was not oriented around the tourist, but around the pineapple! With the 1990 announcement that pineapple plantings would be suspended, Lanai has become totally tourist-oriented.

In 1898, a Harvard graduate named James Drummond Dole got off a boat in Honolulu and saw his future. In 1901, he planted his first pineapple fields on 12 acres of land in Wahiawa. During the two-year wait for the pineapples to ripen, Dole built his own pineapple cannery. After the first harvest was canned and shipped out, Dole's business took off.

In 1922, Dole paid over a million dollars (a staggering sum of money in that era) for the entire island of Lanai, using some of the profit he had made from his Oahu plantation. At the time, it was the largest real estate transaction in Hawaii's history. He bragged to friends later that the island was worth at least $20 million.

Dole converted Lanai, and its 139-square miles of land, into a huge pineapple plantation. He had a harbor built to allow export of the pineapples, and created Lanai City for his workers. Even today, it still looks much like it did when it was first built; a small gridlock of homes surrounded by huge Norfolk pines.

Dole purchased Lanai because its weather is perfect for pineapple growing. It lies in the lee of the West Maui Mountains, which keeps the amount of rainfall it receives low, but at just the right level for pineapples to flourish.

Until recently, the only hotel on the entire island was located within Lanai City. The Hotel Lanai has all of 11 rooms, none of which are equipped with telephones, television or radios. This can truly be called "getting away from it all."

Lanai's newest hotel is the 102-room, $35 million RockResorts Lodge at Koele. In 1991, the Manele Bay Hotel opened its doors to the public.

Maui Air offers affordable island air tours of Lanai, as well as private charters. Call 871-8152 for reservations and information. Aloha Island Air services the island's only airport with its 50-passenger Dash-7 turbo-props. By sea, visitors can travel to Lanai via Expeditions.

If you're coming to Lanai by sea, your first sight of the island will be Manele Bay, a small boat harbor on Lanai's south coast. Once you've docked there, it's just a short journey before you reach nearby Hulopoe Beach. This beach has been designated by the government as a Marine Life Conservation District, which is why the snorkeling here can easily be named among the best in all of Hawaii.

There are only three paved roads on the entire island of Lanai. The rest of the roads are reddish, dusty tracks made (and made flat) by the constant passage of huge pineapple trucks. For this reason, a four-wheel drive vehicle will be necessary if you want to reach many of the historical sites on Lanai. Call Lanai City Service Dollar Rent-a-Car at 565-7227.

The highest point on the island, at 3,370 feet, is Lanaihale. On a clear day, you can see the islands of Maui, Molokai, Hawaii and Oahu from the summit. There is no way to drive up to this lookout; the only way is to hike up the pine-lined Munro Trail, a challenging path that winds in and out of valleys and thick growth. The fantastic reward of Lanaihale's view makes it worth the effort.

While hiking up the trail, you may catch a fleeting glimpse of one of the many animals that inhabit the island. These animals have been brought to the island and left to breed, to provide sport for hunters. You may see goats, turkeys, or even deer trotting through the thick underbrush.

Lanai has several sites where wonderfully preserved petroglyphs can be seen. Luahiwa and Kaunolu Village are two such locations. Finding them is about as difficult as it is to find the other locations on the island. A good map and a good guidebook are necessary equipment, along with a good deal of patience.

On the north end of Lanai, seven miles outside of Lanai City, is the Garden of the Gods. Here, you'll find bizarre lava formations that almost seem to have been created by man. At sunrise and sunset, the rays of the sun shine directly onto the formations, creating a dazzling, almost otherworldly lightshow that would truly be worthy of the gods' attention.

Shipwreck Beach, which runs along Lanai's northern coast, is a solemn testament to the powers of nature. During World War II, many warships ran aground on the jagged reef, driven onto it by the powerful winds that blow through the Pailolo Channel that separates Lanai and Maui. One of these unlucky ships still rests, almost entirely intact, on the reef offshore, and can often be seen from airplanes flying overhead. On the coast and along the beach are the remains of many more ships.

With its growing tourist accommodations and its unique history, Lanai is definitely not an island to ignore — now or in the future.

Lahaina / Lana'i
PASSENGER FERRY

Lahaina Harbor: (Public loading dock in front of Pioneer Inn)
EVERYDAY 6:45 am • 9:15 am
12:45 pm • 3:15 pm • 5:45 pm

Manele Harbor:
EVERYDAY 8:00 am • 10:30 am
2:00pm • 4:30 pm • 6:45 pm

DAILY $25. ONE-WAY

PLAY THE "EXPERIENCE AT KOELE" OR THE "CHALLENGE OF MANELE" GOLF COURSE ON LANA'I
OUR PACKAGE INCLUDES ROUND TRIP TRANSPORTATION FROM LAHAINA ON EXPEDITIONS AND GOLF AT EITHER COURSE.

EXPEDITIONS

**Call for reservations and further information
EXPEDITIONS 661-3756**

Destination
SOUTH SIDE

Ulua Beach near Makena. Photo by Ron Dahlquist.

Wailea is at least three times the size of Waikiki and twice as large as Kaanapali but it doesn't seem that way when you drive through this beautiful community. The reason is seems so small is that construction in the area has been planned out in every detail from the very beginning. Wailea is the perfect example of how to keep growth under control to satisfy residents, and how to best use that growth to satisfy visitors.

Celebrating its 25th anniversary in 1997, Wailea Resort has blossomed along five of South Maui's most beautiful beaches. This 1500 acre resort community hosts five luxury hotels, elegant condominium com-

plexes, three championship golf courses, tennis complexes, restaurants, a shopping village, and private homes among manicured lawns surrounded with mature tropical flowering trees. Everything is clean from the golden beaches to the green grass. Nothing less is expected in Wailea.

Wailea was home to several ancient villages. A heiau can be seen on the golf courses: the designer preserved it and worked it into the design of the courses, providing what has to be the most interesting hazard on any golf course. A few other historical sites are located in Wailea, but they are on private land and not accessible to the general public.

of Fish and Game in 1957, in the hope that nearby ocean life would use the cars to create an artificial reef that would attract the big fish that fishermen look for. The plan didn't work as intended to, but the beach is still beautiful, and the cars provide a unique location for scuba divers in about eighty feet of water.

Mokapu and Ulua Beaches, the protected expanse before the Renaissance Wailea Beach Resort, has plenty of parking, showers and restrooms and being a hotel beach is well maintained with excellent snorkeling out by the first reef.

Wailea Beach is a short but wide expanse with excellent swimming, once the most secluded, now showcases the Grand Wailea Resort.

Polo Beach provides excellent swimming, facilities, and an underwater view of large numbers of fish among the large rocks separating Polo from Wailea Beach.

GOLF

Wailea's condominiums and private residents are discreetly screened from public view by creative landscaping, and the fairways of the three golf courses provide expanses of lush greenery that are markedly different from the areas of dry terrain. The area is a natural desert. The water supply, the most pure on the island, is piped in from the Iao Valley aquifer in a underground aqueduct across the Maui isthmus.

Wailea's Blue, Emerald and Gold Courses are among the top-rated golf links in the United States. These three 18-hole championship courses wind along the lower slopes of Halealaka, overlooking crystal-clear ocean and white sand beaches. The courses change tee and pin placements daily to provide a constant challenge for the golfer.

Set on a hillside above the new Gold/Emerald clubhouse the Wailea Gold training facility simulates the gameplay of the Emerald and Gold courses with several putting, chipping, and target greens, including traps and flags, a driving range that features video instruction, and private lessons and group clinics with Wailea's resident pros.

Both Wailea clubhouses have restaurants, locker rooms, full-service pro shops and preferred rates for guest staying in Wailea. For tee times call Wailea Golf Club (808) 875-5111.

TENNIS

Consistently ranked among the country's top tennis resorts by Tennis Magazine the fourteen courts include eleven plexipaved, three of which are lighted for night. One is a stadium court accomidating 1000 spectators on terraced seating.

The Wailea Tennis Club's staff pros offer a daily range of activities and clinics devoted to various aspects of the game including doubles strategy, ground strokes, volleys, serves, overhead strokes and more. Clinics are limited to six students although one-on-one private lessons are also available. Reservation are a must. (808) 879-1958.

Need a partner? No problem. One of the clubs most popular free services is game arranging. With a pool of over 100 able and willing players and twenty four hours notice the Wailea Tennis Club guarantees a partener to match your skill level.

BEACHES OF WAILEA

Each of the five crescent-shaped beaches that Wailea offers has a unique charm. These little beauties are crescent shaped oasis of white sand that usually end in lava outcroppings at both ends. This makes for sheltered swimmable waters and good snorkeling. Since most of the hotel guests seem to prefer to remain near the hotel pools these beaches are surprisingly uncrowded.

Keawakapu Beach just past the Mana Kai Resort is accessible where South Kihei road dead ends and has plenty of parking but no amenities. Interesting relics in the water about 400 yards off shore include a hundred and fifty junked cars dumped there by the State Department

SOUTH MAUI

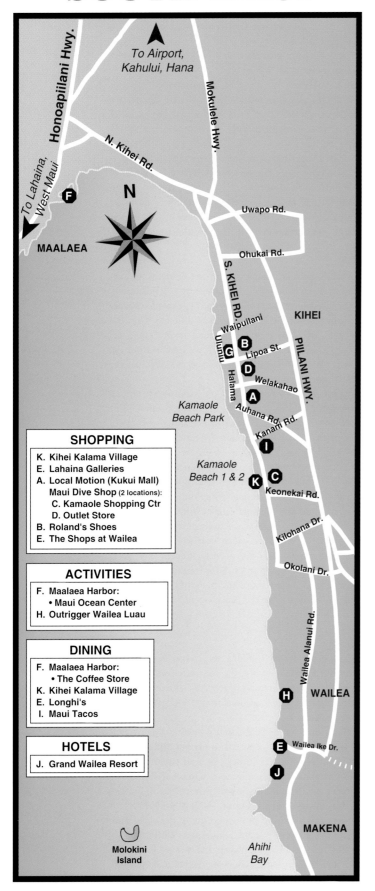

SHOPPING

K. Kihei Kalama Village
E. Lahaina Galleries
A. Local Motion (Kukui Mall)
   Maui Dive Shop (2 locations):
   C. Kamaole Shopping Ctr
   D. Outlet Store
B. Roland's Shoes
E. The Shops at Wailea

ACTIVITIES

F. Maalaea Harbor:
   • Maui Ocean Center
H. Outrigger Wailea Luau

DINING

F. Maalaea Harbor:
   • The Coffee Store
K. Kihei Kalama Village
E. Longhi's
I. Maui Tacos

HOTELS

J. Grand Wailea Resort

Above the pro shop is Joe's Bar & Grill, a casual but elegant restaurant that dishes out "good old American cooking"

Various competative events are hosted throughout the year, including the Wailea Open Championships, one of Hawaii's largest local events. Competitive action is available in one of Wailea's many informal leagues.

ACCOMMODATIONS

Five ocean front hotels: The Grand Wailea Resort & Spa, Renaissance Wailea Resort, Four Seasons Resort, the Outrigger Wailea Resort, and the Kea Lani provide elegant accommodations with full entertainment and amenities.

The Grand Wailea Resort is a feast for the senses with a grand entrance of cascading water falls and sculpted landscapes featuring six independent guest room wings in which most rooms have an ocean view. The pool area features a 2,000 foot river with waterfalls, grottos, slides and rapids. Eight restaurants to satisfy all discriminating tastes include traditional cuisine in the Grand Dining room in addition to specialty restaurants serving Seafood, Japanese, Italian, Family, Snack, Luau and the exquisite fare at the famed Tsunami Nightclub. The opulent 50,000 square foot Spa Grande may well be the most luxurious spa in the world. Camp Grande, a special haven for children, is staffed with qualified personnel and equipped with a children's restaurant, disco, theater, game room, craft room, computer room and much more. The major design themes of flowers, water, trees, sounds, and art create a special place that delights and refreshes.

KIHEI

Kihei, the hottest, driest part of Maui typically gets less than 10 inches of rain a year. Because the arid soil could not be farmed, Kihei was a fairly small community in ancient times. Today, however, due to modern water and electrical engineering, Kihei is the third fastest growing small community in the United States.

Kihei's beaches are unchanged by all the development going around them. They are still long, white, sandy stretches that are perfect for swimming, snorkeling, surfing and more.

Kihei also has the best beach facilities on the island. Almost all the beaches are equipped with showers and restrooms, and lifeguards keep an eye on everyone in the water. There are many places where you can sit down to have a picnic in the warm sunshine. And if you need something, shopping centers are usually just a short walk across the street.

Maalaea Harbor is where Kihei's beach activities begins. The boats docked in the harbor depart daily for snorkeling expeditions, even cruises, fishing charters, whale watches in winter and many other activities.

The breeze that constantly blows through the harbor and the adjacent beaches makes the ocean too choppy for swimming, and the beaches too windy to sunbathe, but windsurfing conditions are great.

In the middle of town the Kalama Beach Park is located in the middle of town and more geared to near-the-beach activities than to actual beach activity. There are many pavilions and tables to picnic on, along with barbecue pits for a picnic. There is also public volleyball, basketball and tennis courts.

With perfect tropical weather, laid back lifestyle, and a

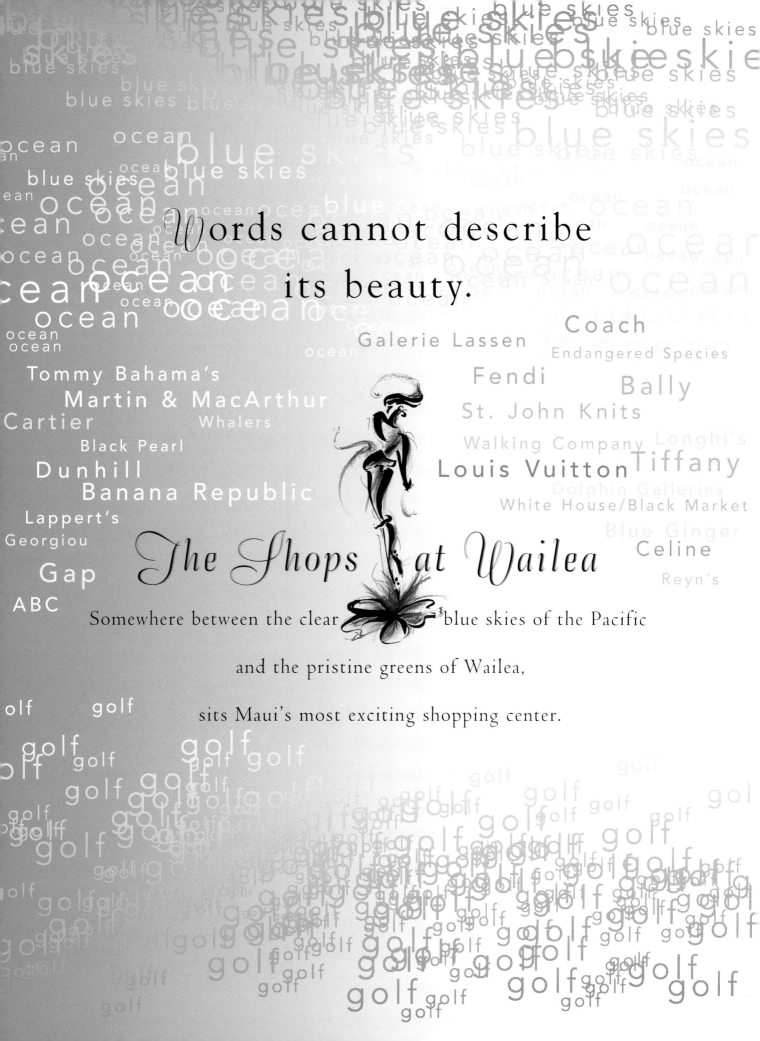

Words cannot describe
its beauty.

ocean

Galerie Lassen

Coach
Endangered Species

Fendi

Bally

Tommy Bahama's
Martin & MacArthur

St. John Knits

Cartier

Whalers

Walking Company

Longhi's

Black Pearl

Louis Vuitton

Tiffany

Dunhill

Dolphin Galleries

Banana Republic

White House/Black Market

Lappert's

Blue Ginger

Georgiou

Celine

Gap

The Shops at Wailea

Reyn's

ABC

Somewhere between the clear blue skies of the Pacific

and the pristine greens of Wailea,

sits Maui's most exciting shopping center.

golf

wide range of shopping and dining opportunities Kihei has become one of the more popular destination for an ever-increasing segment of Maui's visiting population.

MAKENA

Makena has been the most isolated, most quiet part of Maui since it is about as far out of the way as you can get on Maui's south shore.

During the 19th century, Makena Landing was the principle port on the south side that serviced Upcountry Maui. That small landing was eclipsed in the 1920's by Kahului Harbor's modern, centrally-located facilities. With Makena's only real connection to the rest of the world gone, the population shrank to nothing.

Times changed in the 80's with the construction of the beautiful Maui Prince Hotel, an oasis of civilization with gardens, water courses, elegant accommodations and several awarding-winning restaurants all tastefully carved out of the surrounding cactus and kiawe trees.

The two 18-hole Makena Golf Courses, North and South, offer breathtaking views of the Pacific as it's challenging fairways wind around the remains of ancient Hawaiian rock walls along the coastal slopes of Haleakala.

Makena's beaches are among the best on the island, but since they are so secluded, they do not have showers, shelters, or other amenities except for the Naupaka Beach in front of the Maui Prince Hotel.

The second turn off past the Prince leads to Makena's most popular beach: Oneloa Beach, otherwise known as Big Beach; it stretches 3,000 feet down the coastline and remains the largest undeveloped beach on Maui.

If you walk down Big Beach, and scale the cinder cone, you'll find a path that leads to Maui's most infamous beach: Pu'u Olai Beach, known as Little Beach. Because of its seclusion, nude sunbathers favor Little Beach as a place to catch rays au natural.

Beyond Big Beach, where the paved road ends at the beginning of the island's last lava flow two hundred years ago lie the ruins of an ancient Hawaiian fishing village.

The coastal waters are still rich fishing grounds (though fishing is prohibited in the Natural Preserve) and the diving is spectacular with abundant sea life and numerous underwater caves.

Rugged and beautiful, with only a touch of civilization, Makena still offers a taste of Maui much as it used to be.

WELLNESS ON MAUI

Just stepping off the plane onto the island of Maui brings a feeling of well-being to the weary soul. You have arrived to a wondrous destination where many somatic educators and wellness facilitators reside dedicated to providing a nurturing, healing and conscious environment.

Set aside time in your vacation to include a "wellness experience," and pamper yourself on every level – body, mind and spirit. Some of the world's finest healers and spas are located on Maui, so you can easily weave the concept of wellness into the fabric of your visit. You'll return home feeling truly relaxed and refreshed.

For the ultimate spa experience all in one setting, turn to the perennial favorite, Grand Wailea Resort & Spa, located on Maui's south shore, or the newest full-service spa, Hyatt Regency Maui Resort & Spa, oceanfront at Kaanapali Beach.

Bathing traditions from ancient Rome and the Orient are combined with modern-day skin treatments, body massage, and well-

4 NIGHTS WEEKLY

Wailea's Finest Luau

Winner of the Hawaii Visitor's Bureau Kahili Award for perpetuating the essence of Hawaii. Authentic Hawaiian Hula Show complemented with spectacular Luau Buffet and open bar with tropical cocktails. Complimentary shell lei greeting. Wailea's Finest Luau is held on Monday, Tuesday, Thursday and Friday evenings from 5:00 pm to 8:00 pm.

Reservations suggested (808) 879-1922

OUTRIGGER
WAILEA RESORT
MAUI, HAWAII

ness sessions to create the resort spa experience. In recent years, a spa experience was mostly reserved for women; these days, as the Grand Wailea Spa Grande reports, clientele is about 50-50 for both men and women.

Spas often feature a hydrotherapy circuit called, "terme"(which is an Italian term referring to "living waters"). This series of water therapies from around the world forms a prelude to all the massage, facial and body treatments offered in a spa.

Another form of therapy to relax the body is massage. Massage therapy produces healthful benefits. On-site massage has become more popular at deluxe and luxury resorts in recent years. You can even find "massage at the beach" treatments, where a table is set-up under a canopy or a swaying palm tree so you can listen to the sounds of the waves lapping the shore. This is also wellness for the mind.

But the most direct means of eliminating accumulated tension is with an approach called, "somatic education." It improves or restores the natural control of muscular tension by a physical learning process – sort of re-programming the brain. A somatic educator's job is to make it easy for you to regain that control. This approach differs from other methods because it leaves you self-sufficient and able to manage conditions that might otherwise require medical intervention. Thomas Hanna, the developer of Hanna Somatic Education, which is available on Maui, put it this way: "You can live in this high-stress society and avoid the effects of stress, if you take care of yourself properly."

Imagine healing yourself in paradise – ample opportunities for wellness therapy combined with vacation play are available on the island. With the wide variety of services offered, you should first determine whether you are seeking preventative or curative modalities.

For curative relaxation, try the Hawaiian style of massage, known as "Lomi Lomi," which is very soothing to both body and spirit. Or, experience the latest craze, LaStone Therapy – massage with stones. Smooth river rocks are heated, then placed on the body's Chakra points to ground and open the energy centers. The stones are also incorporated into a rhythmic, flowing massage, which is deeply relaxing. If you have a musculoskeletal disorder, then try Hanna Somatic Education; classes are held at Maui Community College, with movement exercises offered on Thursday evenings. These classes are designed to help you prevent stress and tension.

Maui is one of the most powerful healing places on the planet. Use your stay here to control the celebration of your life.

Maui's Most Unique Shopping and Dining Destination

KIHEI KALAMA · VILLAGE

CRAFTS • GIFTS • DINING • ENTERTAINMENT
1941 South Kihei Road across from Kalama Park
Ample free parking in the rear • Open 7 days a week
For more information call 879-6610

NO PAIN, NO PAIN!
• *Back, Neck, or Shoulder Problems* • *Hip Pain*
• *Stiffness* • *General Muscular Discomfort*
Are your plans on Maui disrupted?

"I recently had a severe neck and back problem that was extremely painful. I had one treatment with Cynthia and she alleviated 90% of the pain. I went to her a second time and practically all the pain was gone. It is almost unbelievable how much good she has done for me."
– Robert Mondavi, Robert Mondavi Winery

**Consider Hanna Somatics Education®
with Cynthia Lindway**

• **Improve Mobility, Strength and Coordination**
• **Improve Posture and Appearance**
• **Reverse the "Myth of Aging"**
• **Enjoy more energy**

Unlike other modalities, relief is most often felt within the first fifteen minutes. Maximize your island experience.

Call Today: 879-2227

ADVERTISEMENT

Since the Grand Wailea Resort Hotel & Spa opened its doors in late 1991, its elegant spa has received international acclaim. Spa Grande is proud to hold, for three consecutive years, the distinction of being chosen as the Top Spa Resort in the World by the Readers of Conde Naste Traveler magazine. Spa Grande's multicultural philosophy incorporates traditional Hawaiian healing techniques with the finest European, American, Indian and Asian spa therapies. The award winning Spa Grande, one of the most luxurious spas in the world, helps visitors to achieve optimum health, beauty and a sense of well being.

The signature treatment of Spa Grande is the Terme Wailea Hydrotherapy Circuit. The word "Terme" is derived from the Italian language meaning "living waters." The Terme Wailea Hydrotherapy Circuit is a unique series of international water therapies forming the basis of and prelude to all spa treatments. In the Terme, guests are invited to spend time rejuvenating in the specialty baths, cascading waterfall showers, Roman tub, cool plunges, steam room, sauna, Swiss jet showers and traditional Japanese bath area. Guests in the Terme also receive an invigorating Honey Mango Bath gel loofah scrub to help exfoliate the skin, producing a smooth, healthy and vibrant skin tone. Prior to their spa treatment, guests may relax on the lanai which offers spectacular views of the Pacific Ocean while sipping cool citrus water or ayurvedic tea.

With over 100 treatments to choose from, Spa guests are pampered from head to toe throughout the day. Massage style specialties include Swedish, Hawaiian Lomi Lomi, Lomi

Lomi Pohaku (using nourishing oils and warm lava stones), Reiki, Sports, Jin Shin Acupressure, Aromatherapy, Foot Reflexology, Shiatsu and Thai. Spa Grande treatments range from the embracing warmth of body wraps, rejuvenating facials, indulgent Ayurvedic to the invigorating polish of lymphatic scrubs. Spa Grande has created packages that include well-blended varieties of these world class treatments. Allow the magic of Spa Grande to encompass and sustain the spirit of the Islands, the essence of Aloha, long after receiving this Spa experience kupaianaha (every good feeling you could possibly have)! Relax, replenish, renew!

No great spa would be complete without top-of-the-line cardiovascular and weight training facilities, and Spa Grande's are second to none. Complimented by a staff of the world's finest fitness and aerobic instructors, Spa Grande delivers an unparalleled fitness experience. Start the day with an oceanside power walk, or any one of the fitness classes. Step aerobics, precision cycling, Pilates, Tai chi, boxercise, and yoga are among the classes we offer to assist guests in peaking fitness levels and enhancing great lifestyle choices!

Grand Wailea Resort™
HOTEL & SPA

World's Best Spa Resort

— Condé Nast Traveler Readers' Choice Awards

Enjoying the achievement of your optimum health, beauty and well being is the goal of Spa Grande. This spa is like no other in the world, offering an unequalled facility, a most professional staff and an inspirational beachfront location.

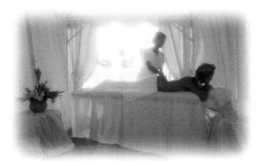

The 50,000 square foot Spa Grande is one of the most luxurious in the world.

Spa Grande™

Grand Wailea Resort Hotel & Spa
3850 Wailea Alanui, Wailea, Maui, Hawaii 96753 Phone: (808) 875-1234

KSL
RECREATION
CORPORATION

Destination
UPCOUNTRY

Upcountry Maui at the 3000-foot level during Springtime when the almost iridescent jacaranda trees, imported from Africa, are in flower. Photo by Jacob R. Mau.

Ascending the slope of Haleakala, one leaves the tropical climes to find land more akin to much of that found in the northwest United States.

As the elevation rises, the temperatures drop — about three degrees for every thousand feet — and the prevailing vegetation reflects the more temperate climate. Deciduous trees and evergreens that seem more appropriate to alpine climes flourish high up the slopes of Haleakala.

Undulating waves of pasture give way to prickly pear on the drier western side, and sugar cane and pineapple are replaced higher up by farms that produce cabbages, onions and many varieties of flowers.

Much of the land Upcountry is ranchland. Cattle, sheep and horses graze the huge tracts known as Haleakala, Ulupalakua and Kaupo ranches.

Amid this beautiful, pastoral setting are the people tending the livestock — Hawaii's cowboys — known here as paniolos.

Towns like Makawao and Kula sprung up long ago to serve the needs of these farms and ranchhands. And, like many of the towns of the Mainland's Old West, these towns' original purpose permeates the streets even today. It's certainly not unusual at any time still to see a rider on horseback clip-clop by. Indeed, the false fronts along the streets of Makawao could serve as backdrops to Hollywood's movies on the taming of the old west.

Inside the Upcountry shops are items not to be found in Lahaina, such as saddles and other tack gear, shirts with pearly buttons, boots with pointy toes, and just to keep our country cousins warm, pot-bellied stoves fueled by wood.

Upcountry is a great place to take a picnic. At the same time you can visit Hawaii's only winery at Ulupalakua Ranch, enjoy the beauty of the protea farms and botanical gardens, catch the classic excitement of a real polo match, hike through a redwood forest, or just enjoy all the magnificent views of Maui.

The scenery may be different, but the aloha spirit is the same with the friendly folks Upcountry. So plan yourself time to visit, and discover another beautiful face of Maui.

Destination
MOLOKAI

The relatively undeveloped, rural island of Molokai, called the "Friendly Isle", maintains many of the old vestiges of Hawaiian spirit.

The Molokai Ranch maintains three distinct recreational areas spread out over 54,000 acres. Deluxe accommodations in bungalow-like tents on platforms, with all modern comforts, are available.

The eastern portion of Molokai is rugged and remote as any area in the state, with deep valleys, plentiful rain and luxuriant waterfalls. Farming and cattle ranching dominate the commerce in the western portion, which is drier with rolling hills and plateaus.

Molokai has a population of only about 8,000 people on 261 square miles with Kaunakakai being the largest town.

Halawa Valley, 30 miles from Kaunakakai, with its spectacular waterfalls, and the lookouts over Kalaupapa peninsula, are outstanding visitor sights. If you are willing and adventurous, there is a mule ride down the steep cliffs to the Kalaupapa settlement, zig-zagging 2,000 feet down along a three-mile route, which is the only way to get there over land.

Perhaps Molokai is best known for being where those suffering from leprosy were taken and forced ashore in the 1860s. Kalaupapa, on the northwest shore, is the community these people developed for themselves under the leadership of the heroic Father Damien.

The "Friendly Isle" can be a fascinating and fun way to feel the real spirit of old Hawaii.

Molokai, the "Friendly Isle", has a windward coast cut by six valleys containing clear, running streams and countless waterfalls. Photo by Ron Dahlquist.

Destination HANA

Abundant vegetation and 56 stream crossings on Maui's tropical windward coast make the drive to Hana unforgettable. Photo by Chris Wayne

Heaven meets the earth in Hana. According to Hawaiian legend, a demigod stood on the crest of Kauiki, a cinder cone that guards Hana Bay, and thrust his spear through the heavens, creating a doorway to Hana.

In ancient times, Hana was a bustling community. Thousands of Hawaiians lived along the coastline. It was so isolated from the rest of the island, it even had its own chieftains.

Hana's proximity to the Big Island of Hawaii also made it important to Maui's warrior chiefs as an important strategic point, where attacks could be launched at Hawaii — and where attacks from Hawaii could be repelled.

This almost constant state of war explains why so many heiau exist along the Hana coast. The heiaus were not just built as places of worship; they were also built as battle monuments.

In the mid-1800s, sugar cane was introduced to the Hana area, but the last plantation closed down shortly after World War II. The population shrank as people left Hana to find employment elsewhere.

The road to Hana is almost as famous as Hana itself. It winds over 52 miles, 617 curves, and 56 bridges, many of which are only one lane wide. The natural wonders unfold as you drive past cascading waterfalls, over deep valleys, and through tropical jungles. During some times of the year, wild ginger blooms alongside the road, providing an intoxicating scent to compliment the intoxicating sights.

Two miles out of Paia is Hookipa Beach, the reason why Paia has become the gathering place for the world's windsurfers. Hookipa is considered to be the best wind-surfing spot in the world. There are very few days where you won't see colorful sails fluttering in the surf offshore.

Keep your eyes on the mile markers planted along the road. Once you pass mile marker 16, you've reached the start of the real road to Hana. From here, the road gets narrower, and curvier. And something unusual occurs; the next mile marker after mile marker 16 starts over at zero. Keep this in mind as you read the directions below.

A half-mile past mile marker 9, you'll see an unmarked turnoff, and a metal turnstile. The turnstile is the beginning of a trail that lets you explore this location, called the Waikamoi Ridge. This is one of the few public trails on Maui, and it is one of the best ways to see Maui's rich jungle plant life.

A bit further down the road, underneath a white bridge, is the Waikamoi Stream. A water fountain near the bridge constantly flows with sweet spring water. While the water from this fountain is safe, you should not drink water from any of the waterfalls or pools.

Puohokamoa Stream is located directly next to mile marker 11. A trail next to the bridge here leads through thick forest down to a pool at the base of a waterfall, and a miniature picnic ground that thankfully includes a covered table in case the rain begins to fall.

Just past mile marker 12 is the Kaumahina State Wayside Park. The park overlooks the beautiful Keanae Peninsula, and includes a picnic area and restrooms.

About two-tenths of a mile past mile marker 16, you'll see an aluminum gate in front of a trail. This trail leads to the Keanae Arborertum. Here, you can view many of Maui's native plants with identification labels.

A sign will steer you on the road down to the Keanae Peninsula. This sleepy town consists of a few homes, some large taro patches, and the Keanae Congregational Church, built in 1860.

Puaa Kaa State Wayside Park is past mile marker 22. There are two small waterfalls, and restrooms — the last you'll find until you reach Hana.

The Nahiku area, near mile marker 25, has a unique history. It became the first rubber plantation in the United States during the early 1900s. The location was too remote and the labor was too costly, so the plantation came to a quick end.

Ka'eleku Caverns, at the 31 mile marker, is a world-class volcanic show-cave. Now open to the public for the first time ever, you can experience a forgotten world, shrouded in mystery, and preserved untouched in absolute darkness under the Hana rainforest for thirty thousand years! Reservations are required for this event. A great family adventure. Call 248-7308.

Waianapanapa State Park is a great location on the road to Hana. This park has a black sand beach, a trail that leads to a heiau and a freshwater cave.

A princess hid in the cave with her handmaiden, trying not to be found by her wicked husband. He found her, and killed both she and her handmaiden. When the water turns red in the cave, this is said to be her blood. It's actually millions of tiny red shrimp that breed in the waters of the cave.

Hana town is very small; don't drive too fast or you'll be leaving town before you know it. Beneath the shadow of Kauiki Hill, native children swim and play in the dark waters of Hana Bay. Legend has it that a commoner, Kauiki, fell in love with a princess, Noenoe. Their love was considered forbidden by the people. A god took pity on the lovers and turned the princess Noenoe into a light, misty rain, and Kauiki into a hill. Even today, in the early morning you can see a misty rain on the brow of Kauiki Hill.

PAST HANA TO KIPAHULU AND BEYOND

Beyond Hana are several small villages, including the villages of Kipahulu and Kaupo.

When the Europeans first arrived in 1778, the picturesque lands of Hana, Kipahulu, and Kaupo were the most densely populated anywhere in Hawaii. Nobles and commoners had chosen this beautiful and bountiful area for their home sites — enticed by the area's lush soil, abundant fresh mountain springs, and nearly perfect climate (created when gentle trade winds push the clouds mauka, toward the mountains, to collect and send down showers, as blessings, at night).

Just outside Hana on the way to Kaupo is the family-owned Hana Herbs & Flowers, growers of exotic herbs and beautiful tropical flowers. They're located up an adventurous four-wheel drive road. Call for an appointment or stop by their bamboo self-serve flower stand at the bottom of the hill 1/4 mile south of Hamoa Beach Road. Owners René and Eileen Comeaux are the first to offer Pohole (fern shoots) for export. Pohole is a great salad food with a delicious taste sensation. They also offer shipping of low cost gift boxes. Call (808) 248-7407 or email hanaherb@maui.net.

The Kipahulu District of Haleakala National Park was established in 1969, to protect the numerous endemic plants and birds.

The Park's remoteness and lack of concessions make it one of the least visited in the U.S., yet perfect for folks seeking a quiet, nature experience.

The Pipiwai Trail takes hikers upstream, along the Pools of 'Ohe'o. Makahiku Falls (185 feet) is one half mile up the trail. Another 1.5 miles up the trail takes one of the base of Waimoku Falls, a spectacular 450 feet straight above. The trail passes through ancient Hawaiian

GOING TO HANA?

For the Horseback Adventure of a lifetime...
Ride with 'Ohe'o Stables
In Kipahulu Valley · 25 Minute Drive Past Hana

Experience the views of Waimoku Falls and Kipahulu Valley you will not see from your car!

Healthy, well kept horses for all levels of riding experience.

*Mention this ad when making reservations for one FREE T-shirt per couple.
*Offer applies only if reservations are booked directly with 'Ohe'o Stables
*No refunds or cancellations with less than 24 hours notice.

Reservations A Must
667-2222

Dawn at Koki Beach near Hana Town, looking toward Alau Island offshore. Photo by Ron Dahlquist.

taro farm sites and through the non-native bamboo forest. The taking of any stone from this area is kapu (strictly forbidden).

'Ohe'o Stables takes small groups of adventurous horseback riders into the Park — a tour for those who wish to get off the beaten path. The trail guides, knowledgeable in Hawaiian traditions and history, take horseback riders approximately two thousand feet up into the mouth of Kipahulu Valley, stopping at the Pipiwai Lookout on the way.

Pipiwai Lookout is a small ridge protruding into the valley, overlooking the bamboo forest. This lookout offers spectacular views of both Waimoku and Palikea Falls. 'Ohe'o Stables guests are served a gourmet lunch while resting at the Lookout.

The late Samuel Pryor, a longtime Kipahulu resident, said it best when he said about Kipahulu: "If ever there was a heaven on earth, this is it."

After Kipahulu, the road continues further around the southern coast of the island, going to Kaupo. The road is unpaved for 4.2 miles, so intelligent driving is a must. The views are some of the finest anywhere, particularly the view of Kaupo Gap. Kaupo Gap was created eons ago when the active volcano of Mt. Haleakala blew away a large section of the crater rim. Refreshments at the bottom of the Kaupo Gap trail are usually available at the historic Kaupo Store operated by the eccentric Manny and Linda Domen.

There's a sense of timelessness in Hana and a sweetness in the air. The aloha spirit of the gentle, graceful people who lived here remains. If there is a heaven on earth, it is here... in Heavenly Hana.

Flowers with the The Spirit Of Aloha!

Fresh & Guaranteed
Free Overnight Shipping
Safe, Secure Online Odering
Or Call Toll-Free 1-800-952-4262

hanaflowers.com

...Our farm to your door.

EXOTIC

KA'ELEKU CAVERNS

One of Maui's best kept secret adventures is now open to all. Maui Cave Adventures at Ka'eleku Caverns in the Hana district, near the Hana airport, offers two very different and incredible hiking tours into one of the largest lava tube systems in the world. The Lava Tube tour is a great family adventure. Nine years and older are allowed on this tour. All participants must be coordinated and in good physical condition as you'll often be hiking on uneven terrain in a completely natural underground setting.

Claustrophobia is hardly a problem, since much of the cave is 40 feet high to the ceiling, and clean, fresh air flows constantly through the cave. Lava tube experts from this family-owned attraction lead small groups daily through what many think may be the best decorated volcanic show-cave anywhere! Adorning the passages are millions of stalactites, incredible drip-castle stalagmites, and gorgeous skylights.

Hana legend claims this underground passage was once a secret tunnel in which runners sent messages and was used over 200 years ago during the warring period before Western Contact. The cave has an average temperature of 67°F, or 19°C, and has been systematically mapped by owner Chuck Thorne and a team from the National Speleological Society.

Unlike water-formed caves on the Mainland and elsewhere, this system was carved by liquid lava which flowed through more than 30,000 years ago. In fact, magma may have flowed in this huge underground conduit for as much as 8,000 years.

For those suspicious of cave hiking, rest assured that this one is State Certified as *not* a burial cave, and the only species of bat in Hawaii does not inhabit lava tube caves.

If you're looking for wild adventure and consider yourself as physically athletic, you won't find any-

Geologic Setting

Maui is the second youngest of the Hawaiian islands, after the Big Island, and was formed with the volcanic rising of Haleakala almost a million years ago. Haleakala is actually the largest of the Hawaiian volcanoes considering that most mass is really under four miles of ocean. The Ka'eleku Caverns were formed in the Hana volcanics in the Haleakala rift zone, which was the last major stage of volcanism on Maui beginning about 100,000 years ago. Topsoil analysis suggests that this cave is about 30,000 years old. A cinder cone above it erupted, the lava flowed down, cooled and hardened on top of the flow while the interior liquid lava outflowed toward the sea plain below, leaving a hollow tube. The last recorded eruption of Haleakala occurred in the early 1790's along the SW rift zone on the opposite side of Maui beyond Makena.

thing on Maui as completely amazing and intellectually stimulating as the two-hour "Wild" cave tour. I'ts like a "journey to the center of the earth"! You need to be 16 years or older for this adventure. On the longer tour there's a fair bit of scrambling over obstacles, ducking, and crawling into pristine side passages. The reward, however, is getting to beautiful passages resembling "ultra smooth chocolate" and other passages colored in blue and gold, from different mineral content.

Come prepared with closed shoes and long pants. At the Ka'eleku Caverns Visitor Center, the friendly and welcoming staff will provide hard-hats, gloves, flash lights, water, and snacks. You'll definitely want to bring your camera, and are likely to get some of the most fun shots of your entire vacation.

Cave tours depart daily and groups are kept small to enhance the eco-experience. Advanced reservations are required; (808) 248-7308. Children 9-17 years must be accompanied by an adult. Visit their website at www.mauicave.com

SEA

A pod of Spinner dolphins cavort off the north shore of Maui. Photo by Dave Fleetham.

*L*ooking down at Maui from high above, the splendid blues and greens of the surrounding coastal waters dazzle the eye, pulling its focus out to sea.

The sea is many things to an islander. The surrounding waters are often a source of food as well as employment. For most people on Maui, it is also the primary source for enjoyment.

Hawaiians have been plying the sea for food, transport and pleasure for centuries. In fact, they are said to have arrived here aboard outrigger canoes centuries before the Europeans were navigating the seas in clipper ships.

Canoes still negotiate the waters here. However, they cut the waters for sport now rather than as the principal means of transportation.

Today's paddlers still take their canoes seriously, though. Championing the racing season here is a considerable source of pride for Maui's canoe clubs.

Hawaiians also cut the waves via surfboards, but they have always done it for sport. Ironically, it has come to be a means of making a living for some nowadays, though even professionals will tell you it is hard for them to consider surfing a "job". It's just plain fun.

Seamen as early as Captain Cook expressed amazement at the graze and enjoyment of island surfers. The aliis, or royalty, would join the common people on solid wooden planks at favorite surfing locations throughout the island and feats on the waves were made famous in song and dance.

Between December and May, boats bring people out to see the humpback whales that come here to perpetuate the species. The whales, of course, have been making the trip to Maalaea Harbor and the leeward waters for years.

There are many other pleasure possibilities for the sea here. One that has caught on in a big way is windsurfing, or sailboarding. In fact, Hookipa, on the windward shore, is recognized now as the best spot in the world to windsurf.

Perhaps the best beaches for swimming and sunbathing on Maui stretch along the coast of West Maui from Kapalua to Olowalu. Kapalua beach is a locals' favorite, good for swimming, snorkeling and bodysurfing, while nearby Napili beach is known for its white sands and fine swimming.

Kaanapali's resort area has a huge white sand beach fronting the hotels with plenty of activities. With over 32 miles of great Maui beaches, your problem may be deciding which to visit first.

Below the surface is another side of Maui's beauty most people miss. The following pages cover snorkeling and scuba, but if you prefer to stay dry check out the deep blue from the comfort of an Atlantis Submarine. Unlike the glass-bottom "subs" that float on the surface, Atlantis Submarines dive 120 feet below the surface to give you a close up view.

WHALEWATCHING

With the arrival of the winter season in December the humpback whales having summered in Alaska and the Bering Sea return to Maui's waters to breed, calf, and tend their young. By late May most have departed. This endangered species is estimated to number fewer than 1500 in the North Pacific region.

Once you've seen them, particularly close-range from the deck of a whale watch cruise boat, you can understand why these gentle giants are so fascinating. A 40-ton adult breaches when it comes bursting out of the water head first. Sentinel whales slap their tails, the strongest muscle in the animal king-dom, on the ocean surface to warn all about the incipient birth of a 15-foot, two-ton infant. Traveling around Maui's coastal waters these playful, air-breathing mammals remind us of the unbelievable variety of natural creatures with which we share our planet Earth.

Maui is a center for observational whale studies through the scientific work of Deborah and Mark Ferrari, who for the last 15 years have developed photographic techniques to identify individual whales by lip groove and fluke (tail) markings as unique as fingerprints. Research continues as to what the song of the male whale singing might signify.

Mother and child humpback whales swimming in the waters off Maui. Their numbers are increasing as worldwide whale hunting declines. Photo by Ron Dahlquist.

SKIM BOARDING

Skimboards are flat, circular-shaped discs about three feet in diameter, used exclusively close to shore. Skim boarders toss their boards onto the shallow water of a receding wave, then race to get a running jump onto the moving board. Board and rider then go "skimming" into the next wave, sending both flipping into the air for some often spectacular acrobatics. It's certainly not for everyone to try, but it's worth seeing. Photo by Maria Veghte.

Maui's beauty
penetrates the
ocean to find
an active play-
ground below
the surface.
Photo by Dave
Fleetham.

DIVING

Maui County's warm, clear waters have some of the best diving in Hawaii. There are literally hundreds of places to stop a car and get into the water. Simply find a safe entry and find yourself in a dazzling environment with incredible life forms, elegant coral formations, and during the winter months, the distant singing of the Humpbacked whales.

SNORKELING

Snorkeling offers fantastic opportunities for viewing the islands' spectacular and abundant marine life. Just beneath the surface of the warm Pacific Ocean are some of the most fascinating and bizarre creatures to be found any place on Earth. Beginning on the surface and sloping down into the abyss are the spectacular reef animals that inhabit Hawaii's tropical seas.

Although most any spot will do, Honolua Bay, Black Rock at Kaanapali Beach, the reef off Olowalu, and Ulua Beach in Wailea are four of the best spots for an amazing diving experience.

Down to a depth of about 30 feet the living coral is most prolific and colorful. Within each coral polyp is an algae that gives the coral its color. The algae and the coral are unable to exist without each other, thus a balance is established that provides for both.

Among the coral branches is a host of shrimp, crabs, and fish found nowhere else. When the coral is taken from the sea, not only does the coral colony die, but also the animals that live among its branches. One of these creatures is a small shrimp that makes a popping noise. Known as the pistol shrimp, it accounts for the crackling sound heard when diving among coral colonies.

For a truly fantastic snorkeling experience, try the short sea excursions to Molokini. The crescent shape of its volcanic rim creates an offshore bay that provides a haven for thousands of spectacularly colored tropical fish. No other island offers the view nor variety of life found here. The rainbow-hued fish that are tame from years of being hand-fed swim around snorkelers in crystal blue water. Porpoise visit year-round, and during whale season, daily sightings of humpbacked whales are common.

Spectacular sail and power boats of all sizes that take snorkelers and scuba divers to Molokini on a daily basis offer first class adventure for the entire family.

TOP TEN REASONS

Why Maui Dive Shop has the Best Snorkeling and Diving Trips to Molokini Crater and La Perouse Bay

LOWEST PRICES & SMALL GROUPS - Our main focus is providing the very best snorkeling and diving available at reasonable prices. We don't have a live band, mixed drinks or buffet lunch and we don't take 50 or 150 people at a time. On our boats, just 24 snorkelers or 18 divers get to comfortably enjoy uncrowded snorkeling and diving. We offer the lowest snorkeling or scuba diving prices to Molokini Crater, Lanaii and La Perouse Bay with no gimmicks, because you book direct with us you save 25-40% over other vendors.

ONLY A SHORT, 15 MINUTE BOAT RIDE - Because our snorkel boats launch from the Kihei small boat ramp instead of one of the boat harbors, it is just a quick boat ride to Molokini instead of the normal 45 minutes. This means you enjoy more time in the water.

COMFORTABLE BOATS - You can choose to be in the sun or the shade. We have onboard restroom facilities and a fresh-water shower to rinse off the salt. The boat is Coast Guard certified and designed for your comfort.

PERSONALIZED SERVICE - Since we take only small groups, everyone gets the attention they need; from snorkeling instruction to help with equipment adjustments or marine life identification. Our crew is there to make this the most enjoyable trip possible. The guide is not there simply as a lifeguard, but to show you to the best areas to see and to point out the highlights and attractions as well as shooting video of you at each location.

MORE SNORKELING & DIVING TIME - We offer, on average, two-and-one-half hours of in-water time on a three-hour snorkel trip. We are able to do this because we have quick boats, so the travel time is short, and small groups so you don't have to wait your turn to enter and exit the water. Our Scuba trips are unhurried and geared toward Hawaiian marine life appreciation.

WE AVOID THE CROWDED TIMES AT MOLOKINI - As you may have seen in pictures, when you get a lot of 60-passenger snorkel boats in the crater, it can be crowded. We avoid this by arriving well before the large boats, and then, as the big boats arrive, we are heading for our second location along the South Maui Coast. On our second trip of the day, we arrive at Molokini about the time that the big boats are departing. Having two destinations adds to your enjoyment by adding variety and keeps you away from the crowds.

SEA TURTLES & MARINE LIFE SPECIMEN SHOW - This is weather dependent, but the south shore of Maui has several locations with an abundance of Sea Turtles and for our second site of the day, we always make the effort to get you there. In addition, our guide will show you marine specimens at each location.

TOP QUALITY EQUIPMENT - Being a dive shop, we use only the best and most up-to-date equipment which we personally fit for you. We also provide wet suits for those who chill easily. This is important! The quality and fit of your equipment can determine how much you enjoy snorkeling or diving.

CHOOSE YOUR TIME OF DAY - We offer two trips daily, one departing at 7 AM for early risers and one at 10 AM for those with a longer drive or for those who prefer to snooze and have breakfast before having fun.

OUR TRIP DOES NOT CONSUME THE WHOLE DAY - Our trips, while giving you all the water time you want, still leave you time to enjoy activities for the rest of the day. PLUS ... A friendly, helpful, and professional boat crew. AND you also get Bad Ass Kona coffee, cinnamon rolls, juice, soda, beer and snacks.

MAUI DIVE SHOP • 6 LOCATIONS, ISLAND WIDE

Molokini or La Perouse Snorkel Cruise

$39 No Gimmicks

FREE Dive Guide

Stop by any one of the 6 Maui Dive Shops to pick up your FREE Maui Dive Guide. Containing detailed full color maps to all the best snorkel and dive spots.

MAUI DIVE GUIDE

SNORKEL RENTAL
Lowest Prices Guaranteed From **$1**49

Rent snorkel equipment from $1.49 a day or rent our Deluxe Package (Silicone Mask, Dry Impulse Snorkel, Fins, Mesh Bag, De-Fog, Fish Card, Plus Free Dive Guide) and receive a Free Snorkel Cruise or $10 Off our $39 Molokini Snorkel Turtle Cruise.

FREE SNORKEL TURTLE CRUISE

SNORKEL/ACTIVITY COMBOS:

Maui Dive Shop combines their Molokini Snorkel Cruise with other great Maui activities at one low price. (Prices subject to change)

FIRE & WATER
Award-winning Maui Marriott Luau and Molokini Snorkel Cruise.
$94

$165

ABOVE & BELOW
A 45-minute flight with Sunshine Helicopters and Molokini Snorkel.

NIGHT & DAY
Dining and dancing aboard the 118' luxury yacht Maui Princess and Molokini Snorkel Cruise.
$105

MAUI DIVE SHOP
6 STORES ON MAUI

Lahaina
661-6166

HONOKOWAI MARKETPLACE
LAHAINA CANNERY MALL
WHALERS VILLAGE
KAHANA GATEWAY CENTER

Kihei
879-3388

1455 S. KIHEI ROAD, KIHEI
(OUTLET STORE)
KAMAOLE CENTER, KIHEI

www.mauidiveshop.com

MAUI'S FASCINATING

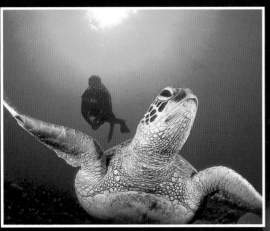

One of the resident 4' long Green Sea Turtles found off the Hyatt Regency in Kaanapali at the 35 foot level.

A crab carries two anemones which use stinging cells to subdue prey for both.

Pair of 3' Dragon Eels in reef side of Molokini crater. These night feeding carnivorous morays remain territorial near their 40' deep coral crevices.

Mollucan Angler Fish, preferring to remain camouflaged on the bottom, uses the spine on dorsal fin as fleshy bate lure.

Second cathedral of Lanai at 50 ft.:

UNDERWATER WORLD

PHOTOS BY DAVE FLEETHAM

Slate-pencil urchins, which live in hollow coral reef pockets, have an external skeleton with blunt spines which fall off easily.

Day Octopus at 40' off Lanai is usually camouflaged on the bottom. With eight muscular arms and very good eyesight, these mollusks without a shell are the most intelligent of all animals without a skeleton.

When threatened, Puffer Fish suck in a belly full of water to grow three times in size. This carnivorous fish, whose outside skin feels like Velcro, uses its sharp beak to crush small prey. Even though the internal organs contain tetrodotoxin, a deadly nerve poison, in Japan related species prepared by certified chefs are eaten with great relish in a gourmet dish called 'fugu'.

a safe dive with many exits.

the island are trade winds that originate in the northeast and provide ideal offshore or side wind surfing conditions along the north, south and west shores. But on the eastern shore, the trades can cause bumpy surface conditions.

Kona winds result from the occasional storm that sends warm winds toward Hawaii from the South Pacific, producing the opposite effect of tradewinds. The north, south and west shores will be bumpy while the eastern shores should be ideal.

Of course the local geography may alter the effect of the winds on individual beaches despite the general patterns. The direction of the swells reaching the island is another important factor in determining where the best surfing beaches will be on a particular day.

Hawaii's waves are much more powerful than those that reach the mainland due to the lack of continental shelf to slow them down. Because of that, anyone unfamiliar with the surf should use caution.

The ancient Hawaiians found surfing to be a great opportunity to enjoy the ocean and be together as equals, regardless of their status. The royalty and the common people both found surfing to be a thrill, as do thousands around the world today.

A great place to start your adventure into the sport of surfing is Local Motion. Top-quality surfboards and equipment are available for sale or rent, and the friendly staff can advise you on where to find the best surf to match your abilities. They also have the largest selection of contemporary clothing which best represents the Hawaiian surf lifestyle. Visit one of their four convenient locations and find out why Local Motion is Hawaii's favorite surf shop.

The thrill of surfing is easy to imagine when watching a skilled surfer carve and hop across the surface of a wave. Ryan Jung photo by Eric Aeder.

SURFING
SPORT OF THE HAWAIIANS

Surfing is a sport as native to the islands as the ancient Hawaiians, who were drawn to the sport in droves for its simplicity and excitement. The aliis, or royalty, would join the common people on solid wooden planks at favorite surfing locations throughout the island and feats on the waves were made famous in song and dance.

Today, the excitement and thrill of surfing has not diminished. Thousands of surfers are drawn to Maui's coastlines in search of ideal waves.

Waves arrive in two seasons. Summer's south swells wrap around the southern part of the island and are smaller waves that average two to five feet. The winter season, October to March, marks the coming of the north swells, when waves average four to eight feet and often top ten to twelve feet.

Wave characteristics are generally dependent upon reef shape and wind conditions, which account for the varying shape, power and thrust of waves at different break locations.

Two basic types of wind affect surfing waves, trade winds and Kona winds. Ninety-five percent of the winds that reach

MAUI'S HOTTEST SURF SPOTS

Great surfing can be found at most beaches on Maui, depending on the season.

In summer, local surfers head to the south shores of Maalaea, where small, fast, hollow waves are held up by steady wind, and Olowalu, known for a sandy bottom and small, easy-to-ride waves.

The Lahaina Breakwall, in view of historic Lahaina, gets 2-8 foot waves and is usually best at high tide. Nearby Lahaina Harbor is the site of The Lahaina Surf Classic, Local Motion's annual summer contest, where Maui's hottest amateur surfers from around the island compete.

During winter a favorite north shore surfing beach is Honolua Bay, known as the best for near-perfect tubes that hold size. Other good winter surfing beaches are Paukulauko, best during strong Kona winds and Ho'okipa, with large waves intensified by strong winds and currents.

Remember these aren't the only great surf beaches on Maui, only some of the best.

Featuring the largest selection of contemporary clothing that best represents the Hawaiian surf lifestyle. Visit one of our four convenient locations and find out why Local Motion is Hawaii's favorite surf shop.

Local Motion

Where Aloha Is Always In Style

MADE IN HAWAII

• 1295 Front St. in Lahaina **Tel. 661-7873**
• Lahaina Center **Tel. 669-7873**
• Kaahumanu Center in Kahului **Tel. 871-7873**
• Kukui Mall in Kihei **Tel. 879-7873**

Ocean Awareness

Maui is blessed with an environment remarkably free of hazards common in the most of the world. There are no snakes, dangerous large mammals or reptiles and no poison oak or ivy. However if you snorkel or dive the potential for injury exists.

The basic safety rule is don't turn you back on the ocean and watch where you put your hands and feet! Most injuries involve getting cut by a sharp coral or the occasional encounter with a minding-its-own-business creature.

For those with a strong immune system: clean the wound, apply hydrogen peroxide, antiseptic or a topical antibiotic and keep clean. Remember, all ocean water worldwide contains a mix of micro organisms. Always clean any wound after leaving the water. Above all remain calm.

Shark attack is uncommon in Hawaii although every one has the fear. Avoid swimming in unclear water especially near stream outflows after storms.

Portuguese Man of War and Jelly Fish are rarely a problem here but they can blow near shore from southern or Kona winds. The long blue tentacles trailing below the jelly-like floating body is alive with stinging cells which cause severe burning pain on contact, and sometimes blistering. Remove the tentacles with something other than bare hands such as tweezers, driftwood or sand. To neutralize the stinging cells and reduce the pain use vinegar, diluted household ammonia or meat tenderizer, all of which denature the protein which causes the pain reaction.

Sea Urchins are almost stationary globe creatures with a hard stone like skeleton outside their living tissues usually covered with sharp spines. If you accidentally step on one of these, spines can break off and leave a foreign body. To control the throbbing pain immediately soak the area in hot, not scalding, water up to 90 minutes. Undiluted vinegar soaking is effective for dissolving small spine fragments. Massive punctures, especially near a joint, will require the attention of a physician.

Eels are nocturnal creatures that are occasionally seen during the day poking their heads out of rock and coral. They rarely bite, and then only if mistakenly provoked. Like most creatures they do not want trouble and prefer to retreat. However if you are accidentally bitten it is usually painful because of sharp teeth. To treat, clean and apply antibiotic. Large bites require medical attention for stitches and antibiotics.

Coral is a living creature with a hard skeleton containing a colony of organisms that contain immuno reactive proteins in addition to ocean bacteria. Coral should never be touched or walked upon, but if a scrape occurs immediately clean with hydrogen peroxide, or soap and water. The wound will take several days to heal. Clean and treat with hydrogen peroxide every time you return from the ocean until the skin surface seals over and no redness on the wound edges appears.

Escape to Paradise

Let the Best of Maui bring you back to paradise. It's the perfect souvenir of your trip, and the perfect gift for friends and family!

Only $15 for the full-color, hardbound edition, including shipping by air (in U.S. and Canada).

Send check, money order, or credit card number with expiration date to: Best Of Maui, P.O. Box 10669, Lahaina, HI 96761 or use the card between pages 132 and 133.

www.bestofmauiguide.com

Foreign orders sent by surface. All payment in U.S. funds.

BEST OF
MAUI
SPORTS · RECREATION · DINING · SHOPPING

AIR

by land. Every visitor to Maui deserves to see them, but how can they?

By taking to the skies. Air tours allow you to "flightsee" the island, getting a bird's-eye view of practically every major location on the entire island, along with many locations that you wouldn't see any other way.

Just about all of the major helicopter tours, as well as Active Volcano Air Tours, explore the three major regions of the island — the West Maui Mountains, East Maui, and Haleakala Crater. Some tours even take passengers over two of the other islands of Maui County, Lanai and Molokai.

The West Maui Mountains are the remnants of one of the volcanoes that eventually formed Maui. These mountains separate Lahaina and Kaanapali from Wailuku and Kahului. The Honoapiilani Highway curves along the coastline, so the mountains are completely inaccessible by car. In the air, however, you'll see the beauty that shines within this mountain range.

Puu Kukui, the largest mountain in the entire range, is the second wettest spot in the United States. An average of more than 400 inches of rain falls here over the course of just one year! Because of this constant precipitation, the West Maui Mountains teem with many waterfalls that simply cannot be seen unless you are airborne.

In addition, the constantly running water has worked down the mountains over time, creating fantastic valleys and canyons.

The Iao Valley, located in Central Maui, can't be forgotten. From the air, you can see that Iao Needle is one end of a much larger ridgeline, and much less imposing than it is from the ground. This 2,000-foot-plus monolith was created by the same natural forces that carved, and continue to carve, valleys into the West Maui Mountains.

An air tour over-flight is the most efficient way to see much of the beauty of Maui. Honolua Bay Marine Preserve north of Kapalua. Photo by Ron Dahlquist.

Maui is not considered a very large island by geological standards; it covers only 729 square miles of land. For a visitor, however, the main concern is not how many square miles there are, but how to see as many of those square miles as possible.

Doing this from the driver's seat of a car isn't as easy as it seems. There are many beautiful locations on Maui that can't be reached or even seen by car, or

Nestled close to the Iao Valley is the Waihee Valley. This valley is thought to be the first place on Maui where the ancient Polynesians settled, between 500 and 700 A.D.

Unbelievably, these ancient settlers traveled between the West Side and Iao Valley by hiking through the West Maui Mountains. Very few hikers nowadays will even attempt this test of strength and stamina.

As spectacular as the West Maui Mountains are,

they almost pale in comparison to the majesty of Haleakala Crater. This long-dormant volcano is perfectly suited to flightseeing; the same incredible size that makes the Crater so amazing also makes it impossible to fully enjoy the experience of seeing it when you're stuck on the ground.

Molokai has its spectacular north shore, with the massive cliffs, verdant valleys, waterfalls and Kalaupapa peninsula. Lanai has its renowned resorts, pineapple fields and Shipwreck Beach. Kahoolawe (a 50-year military bombing target) is undergoing a massive government cleanup in its return to the State of Hawaii for use as a Hawaiian cultural site. Molokini, with its sunken crater, is known for snorkeling. These can all be seen from Maui by Maui Air at 871-8152.

Your visit to Maui would not be complete without seeing the "Big Island", as it is known locally. It has been formed by five volcanic rift-zones. The oldest, in Kohala, is inactive; Hualalai, which last erupted in 1801, and Mauna Kea (at 13,796 feet) are probably dormant; Mauna Loa (at 13,680 feet) and Kilauea, still very much awake, are the most active volcanoes on earth. The Big Island is the youngest island and is still growing thanks to the virtually continuous volcanic activity of Kilauea rift-zone.

An air tour is the only way to see the cliffs, valleys and waterfalls of the Kohala Mountains, the rain forests on the slopes of Mauna Kea, the world's largest mountain of Mauna Loa, the world class observatories on the top of Mauna Kea (and

even snow in the winter) and especially the activity of the world's most prolific volcano where red lava is seen most of the time. This can all be seen in approximately two hours on Volcano Air Tours comfortable, multi-engine airplanes. You can depart from two convenient locations: at the main airport in Kahului, and at the Kapalua-West Maui Airport, just a few miles from Kaanapali and Lahaina.

An overflight is the easiest way to view Haleakala's 10,023-foot summit overlooking the dormant volcano. Photo by Ron Dahlquist.

Let ALEXAIR show you... the Best of Paradise!

ALEX AIR
ALL-STAR HELICOPTERS
www.helitour.com

Flights as low as $69

Daily Flight Specials
871-0792

Maui's Museums

Experience Maui from another time. Considering the geographical remoteness and unique natural and cultural history of Hawaii the more than 70 museums and cultural attractions in the State provide residents and visitors an opportunity to be acquainted with fascinating aspects of how we came to be. These privately-funded Maui destinations welcome your visit.

The Brig Carthaginian in Lahaina Harbor is a simple floating museum reminding all of the once primitive transport to Maui.

LAHAINA

LAHAINA RESTORATION FOUNDATION
Walking tour. Over 200,000 visitors in 1998.

The foundation supports four Lahaina cultural attractions: The Baldwin Home, Brig Carthaginian, Wing Ho Temple and the House of Printing. The main offices are located in the Baldwin House on Front Street. Archival collections of books, documents, and photos are housed. The Foundation also maintains the Seaman's Cemetery, the Plantation House, the old Lahaina Lighthouse, and the Hale Pa'ahao (the former prison on Prison street now used for community meetings).

WHALERS VILLAGE MUSEUM
Whalers Village, Kaanapali
Daily 9:30am-10pm, Free. (808) 661-5992.
Over 500,000 Visitors in 1998.

Whales and whaling history are showcased. Outdoor exhibits include a 40-foot sperm whale (origin of perfumery treasure ambergris) and an authentic whaleboat. Inside on second floor exhibit include large scale model of a whaling boat, a recreated ship forecastle and detailed exhibit describing the arduous life of mid-19th century whaling life. Gift shop

UPCOUNTRY

HUI NO'EAU VISUAL ARTS CENTER
2841 Baldwin Avenue, Makawoa
Mon-Sat 8am-4pm, Free admission.
(808) 572-6560. Over 30,000 visitors in 1998.

The art center is located in a 1917 plantation mansion once the home of the organization's founder Ethel Baldwin. Continually changing exhibitions feature contemporary traditional, national and international art from established and emerging artists. Gift shop features unique works by hui members including fine art, jewelry, and crafts.

Bailey House Museum in Wailuku.

HANA

HANA CULTURAL CENTER
4974 Uakea Road, Hana
Daily 10am-4pm, $2. (808) 248-8622
About 15,000 visitors in 1998.

Offers an authentic thatched housing complex and gardens to stroll through. A village consisting of a men's meeting house, a sleeping house, a cooking house and a canoe house all dedicated in 1996. The gardens showcase several different varieties of taro as well as plants for food, medicine and shade. A gift shop offers local crafts, gifts and books.

CENTRAL MAUI

MAUI OCEAN CENTER
Maalaea Harbor
Daily 9am- 5pm. (808) 270-7000

Hawaii's largest state of the art open ocean aquarium covers 5 acres with over 40 aquarium exhibits featuring the indigenous fish to Hawaiian waters.

Much of the center is designed to allow you to walk through clear underwater viewing tunnels. The white translucent jelly fish in the cylindrical transparent tank, rare grass eels, and phosphorescent glowing coral remind you that the ocean is another parallel world.

The daily feeding frenzy at 10:30 and 3:30 in the shark tank is a must see. Divers are visible maintaining the tanks, with sting ray feeds at 12:30 and 3:00. The Sea Turtle Lagoon and the Whale Discovery Center answer many questions about these large creatures.

The park also features the Seascape Restaurant and several ocean-theme gift shops.

BAILEY HOUSE MUSEUM
2375A Main street, Wailuku
244-3326
Mon-Sat 10am-4pm, $4 Adults.
(808) 244-3326. Over 15,000 visitors in 1998.

Chronicles the early 1800's missionary days and houses unique Hawaiian pre-contact artifacts: a striking Lono amakua, jewelry, weapons and an excellent archival collection of photographs and illustrations by appointment.

MAUI OKINAWA CULTURAL CENTER
688 Nukuwai Place, Wailuku
Mon-Tues 9am-12noon; Wed/Thurs/Fri 8-11am
Free. (808) 242-1560
Free, Number of visitors in 1998: 500

Houses artifacts and personal items from the first generation Okinawans who came to Maui for plantation work.

ALEXANDER & BALDWIN SUGAR MUSEUM
3957 Hansen Road, Puunene
Mon-Sun 9:30am-4:30pm, $4. (808) 871-8058
Over 30,000 visitors in 1998.

Everything concerning the history of the product that helped re-populate the Hawaiian Islands in the 19th century. Machines, water works, scientific agriculture and immigrants created the highest yielding sugar lands in the world.

HAWAII NATURE CENTER
875 Iao Valley Road, Wailuku
Daily 10am- 4pm, $6 adults, $4 Children.
(808) 244-6500

The Iao Interactive Science Arcade includes 30 hands-on exhibits designed for children to the explore Maui's tropical natural environment. Guided nature walks are offered daily with advanced reservations

PAPER AIRPLANE MUSEUM
Maui Mall on Kaahamanu Ave., Kahului.
Free admission.
Maui aviation history from 1910 to today in a pleasant shop run by Ray Roberts, a retired school teacher. Paper model kits for sale.

The Sugar Museum maintains a meticulous collection about Maui's plantation history.

Maui's Gardens

While some popular media report about the loss of rainforest and extinction of plants, Maui continues to be covered with a remarkable variety of wonderful, attractive, unusual, and useful plants from sources around the world. Tradition holds that the original Polynesian voyagers brought about 30 plants new to Hawaii in canoes over a thousand years ago.

New specimens continue to arrive, and thrive, since the Maui climate has 11 of the world's 13 zones. You can visit these public destinations to appreciate the variety of plant life that can grow and propagate when the temperature never reaches freezing. Unique species of plants, found only in Hawaii before any human arrival, are losing habitat space as lands are cleared and new plants fill the clearings. Like the peoples of Hawaii, our plant populations are evolving from the abundant worldwide variety of tropical plants.

Photos by David B. Fleetham

CENTRAL MAUI

MAUI TROPICAL PLANTATION
Waikapu

This working plantation on 60 acres features tropical fruit trees: papaya, banana, cherymoya, mac nut, citrus, pommelo, oranges, limes, coffee, ginger, star fruit, pineapple, mango and ornamental flowers all easily accessible from a narrated 40-minute tram ride that departs every 45 minutes.

KEPANIWAI HERITAGE GARDENS
Free, 7am to 7pm. On the Iao Valley Road next to the Hawaii Nature Center.

Traditional Hawaiian and other culture pre-contact living structures. Examples of Hawaiian pili grass housing. Bring a picnic and enjoy in shelters that line the Iao stream.

TOWARD HANA

KAHANU BOTANICAL GARDENS
ETHNOBOTANIC GARDENS
On Ulaino Road off the Hana Highway before Hana Airport road. 248-8912.

Features 123 acres of gardens dedicated to the study, propagation and conservation of the world's tropical plants with labeled trees, including 120 varieties of breadfruit. Special emphasis is on plants of the Pacific islands. The oceanfront Piilanihale Heiau is the State's largest and best preserved archeological site and shown by regular guided tour.

KEANAE ARBORETUM
Beyond the half way road to Hana. Free admission.

State park featuring ornamental ginger, heliconia, fruit trees and shrubs are clearly marked with identifying labels. Walk the mile length to see the stream water course with functioning taro fields.

GARDEN OF EDEN
Located between mile marker 10 & 11 on road to Hana. 280-1912. Admission $4. Mon-Sat 9am-2pm.

Explore 25 acres of nature trails planted by landscape designer Alan Bradbury. Located 26 miles (about 50 minutes) from Kahului, this is an area of low elevation tropical jungle with 150 inches of rainfall per year. Think of the opening sequence of the movie Jurassic Park.

UPCOUNTRY

KULA BOTANICAL GARDENS

Highway 377 a mile above Highway 37 junction in Kula. Adults, $5; Children 6-12, $1; under 6, free. Open daily 9am-4pm. 878-1715.

Located on 5.5 acres situated at 3,300-foot elevation in the perpetual spring of Kula. This high garden showcases orchids, proteas, bromeliads and rare Hawaiian trees. The upper reaches are the source of Maui grown Christmas trees sold during early December.

TEDECHI VINEYARD
Ulupalakua

On the road toward Hana via the back road way, toward Kaupo, about 5 miles from upcountry Kula, is a pleasant oasis of Norfolk pines at the Ulupalakua ranch. The solid white coral tasting room offers samples from Hawaii's only grape vineyard planted in the Carnelian grape, used for making Maui Red table wine. Novelty pineapple wine is also available.

HALEAKALA NATIONAL PARK
(808) 572-9306

The 27 miles of trails covers a land of sudden contrasts in terrain, topography, and weather with several different trails available.

HOSMER GROVE, a living tree museum at the edge of the Halealaka Park on the road to the summit (route 378), has a half mile trail in an easy 30-minute, self-guided hike. The 20 species of alien trees were planted in Hawaii as an uneconomic experiment in timber farming. The signage throughout the path explains the on-going efforts to preserve Maui's native forests.

VISITOR CENTER on the highway inside the park houses a collection of detailed maps along with animal, plant, and mineral exhibits. One look down into the crater from the summit will confirm that descent into the cinder trails requires planning and rugged hiking equipment. Limited cabin space and overnight stays are available with reservations.

WAIKAIMOI PRESERVE hikes are scheduled Monday and Thursday mornings at 9am, beginning at the Hosmer Grove and lead by the Park Service. Reservations: 572-9306. Second Saturday of each month a hike is lead by the Nature Conservancy (572-7849). Waikaimoi is a fenced preserve of native and rare Hawaiian species with windswept sub-alpine regions, original rainforests of koa and 'ohi'a trees, and rare birds.

LAHAINA

KAPALUA GUIDED TOURS
Kapalua Resort Activity Desk, 669-8088. $26.

Twice daily, Monday through Friday, 2.5 hour guided tours into the pineapple fields will teach you the history of this Central American fruit and allow you to pick your own.

A lottery system and $500 fee buys a seat on a helicopter taking you to the top of Pu'u Kukui—the tallest wettest place on Maui. On a clear August day this once-in-a-lifetime experience takes you to the pygmy bog forest and a two-mile hike on a boardwalk path through these closed kapu lands. (During Ecotourism week open one day each year)

Other West side outdoor expeditions lead by Attitudes and Latitudes, 661-7720, include: Hike to the 70 year old MAUNALEI ARBORETUM, planted with mature and rare specimen trees from the world's tropical belt, and continue to the top of Pu'u Ka'eo (1,635-foot elevation) to view the incredible panorama over Kapalua. The roundtrip, $70 hike covers 1.75 miles and takes 4 hours from 8am to noon.

KAHAKULOA VALLEY AND NAKALELE SEA CLIFFS EXCURSION from 8am-2pm covers a region of ocean blow holes to a tropical rainforest valley. This popular $110 per person trek covers 4 miles of moderate difficulty.

National Tropical Botanical Garden.

Randy Hufford

Mango, The King of Fruits with irresistible flavor originally from India is available all summer. A mature tree will produce 1000 pounds of fruit. Best trees from Lahaina to Kihei.

Randy Hufford

Joe Harabin

Papaya, Favorite breakfast melon-like fruit from a fast growing herbaceous tree. 45 species form fruit from palm size to 8 lb giants.

The Kahanu Gardens near Hana, a satellite garden of the extensive National Tropical Botantical Garden in Kauai, contains a collection of Hawaiian plants and a complete collection of Breadfruit trees. One such tree can provide enough food for a family all year; yet this delicious staple has never been popular outside southern Polynesia.

Tropical

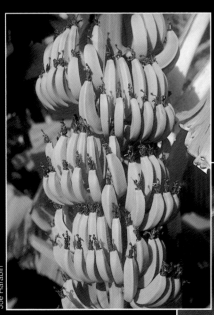

Joe Harabin

Banana, Fruit of paradise which ripens all year is America's most popular fruit. Original Hawaiians brought live plants by canoe. There are 70 varieties including red, apple, dwarf, and cooking.

Randy Hufford

Randy Hufford

Coconut, The coco palm tree, which is the staff of life for many islanders, grows best near sea level. Each tree yields 50 coconuts a year which take 10 months to ripen. Every part used: food, oil, fiber, fuel, containers, shade.

Randy Hufford

National Tropical Botanical Garden.

Randy Hufford

Macadamia Nut, Native tree of Australia produces round hard nuts all year. Mature trees produce over 100 pounds/ year.

National Tropical Botanical Garden.

Coffee Originally from the Ethiopian highlands, this flavorful mental stimulant has been planted in West Maui and Kona in order to take advantage of premium prices for specialty coffees.

Most of the important tropical fruits can be found growing at the Maui Tropical Plantation in Central Maui. Admission is free and a tram tour is available for a small additional fee. You can purchase a variety of fruits to take home, or enjoy them at their Tropical Restaurant.

Fruits

National Tropical Botanical Garden.

Star Fruit, Translucent yellow stars on ornamental trees from China produce sweet, juicy fruits which keep well when dried.

Pineapple, This symbol of hospitality requires 20 months to ripen. Yield in Hawaii is13,000 fruits per acre. All pineapples in Hawaii are the same type, Smooth Cayenne.

Ron Dahlquist

Randy Hufford

Jacob Mau

Hibiscus, the Hawaii state flower originally from the Caribbean, come in all colors up to 10" across.

Orchids, originally imported from tropical America are among the most evolved and diverse plants on earth. Most need no soil and obtain nutrition from rainfall.

Jacob Mau

Tahitian Ginger, which grows on a single stem directly from the soil, makes a long lasting cut flower. *Photo by Jacob Mau*

Heliconia purpurea, the lobster claw, is from the banana family, one of 80 species from tropical America.

Jacob Mau

Plumeria, useful for simple aromatic leis, is grown on an easily propagated tree.

Jacob Mau

of Maui

Hanging Heliconia, the large, waxy, hanging flowers originally from Peru, maintain their color for over three weeks.

Ron Dahlquist

Bird of Paradise, a Hawaiian trademark flower, is also part of the banana family and native to Africa.

Jacob Mau

Heliconia wagneria is one of the loveliest spring flowering blossoms.

Jacob Mau

Protea flowers are originally from South Africa and come in 1400 varieties growing on the Upcountry slopes of Kula flower farms.
Photo by Jacob Mau

Silversword, found only in high elevations of Haleakala, is a member of the sunflower family that can survive for years without rain.

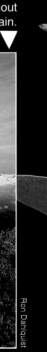

Ron Dahlquist

Hawaiian Leis

Text by Karee Carlucci

Leis are a symbol of love in the giving of them, and leis say "Aloha" back to the world when you wear them. In Hawai'i, past and present, leis are worn for ornamentation as necklaces (lei 'a'i), or on the head (lei po'o). Share the aloha.

Yellow-orange Lantern 'Ilima and white Tuberose are strung together to create a popular lei with a nice twist. The 'ilima flower represents the island of O'ahu. Another style of lei is made from 'ilima papa, by stringing together hundreds of these paper-thin petals into a smooth rope, known as the Royal Ilima. Tuberose flowers are found clustered on a tall stalk and emit a very sweet fragrance.

RON DAHLQUIST

A variety of flowers and leaves arranged and woven into a lei is known as haku style. You can see this style, as pictured left, on head leis. Leaves from the ti plant are frequently twisted and tied into ropes with rosettes added (right) to create a strong, long-lasting lei. The ti leaf symbolizes good luck.

The exotic Jade vine produces lovely seed pods which are blue-green in color, and makes a stunning necklace. Jade is available from late Spring to early Summer, but is not allowed to travel out of the islands because of the seeds. The combination seen here is with clusters of Tuberose.

Fragrant petals of the White Ginger flower are painstakingly woven with their stems, creating a delicate lace-like pattern on the inside with the blossoms on the outside. This necklace can be used for brides and should be worn laying flat like a collar. Its spicy-sweet fragrance is light and heavenly

Lei stands can be seen at the Honolulu International Airport and along country roads. You'll find Lei Ladies attending the stands and stringing flowers while you watch. The most common varieties of lei are strung with Carnations and Tuberose (red, pink and white), Plumeria blossoms (yellow and white), and Dendrobium Orchids (purple and white). While orchids do not usually emit a scent, carnations, tuberose and plumeria each have their own distinctive fragrance.

RON DAHLQUI

The traditional art of gathering seeds from trees and shrubs and stringing them into endless combinations of lei has been making a big comeback. These seed leis are found at arts and crafts fairs, as well as in hotel lobbies and shopping centers which feature cultural arts exhibits. Types of seeds used include Wiliwili, Kukui nut, and Job's Tears.

RON DAHLQUIST

Maile leaf is very revered in Hawai'i and found growing on vines in the rain forest. You can recognize it by a delicate spice scent and shiny dark green leaves. The maile lei is twisted into a rope which hangs open, and is used for different special occasions. It's often worn by the groom in a wedding, and is symbolic at the opening blessing of a new business. A maile lei should not be cut, just untied.

The Kukui (or candlenut) tree grows a nut the size of a small walnut, which can be found in an array of colors. When young, the nutshell is white and as it ages, it turns darker to almost black. Kukui is the state tree of Hawai'i, and leis are made from its silvery maple-like leaves, as well as from the nut. Combinations of Kukui nut leis are found everywhere.

'Ohai Ali'i is the name of this lei, coming from the Royal Poinciana or Flame Tree. The dense clusters of red blossoms include a white or yellow petal, which bloom from Spring through Summer, and the long brown pods hold seeds that are also made into leis.

Palapalai Fern is a favorite of lei makers, especially for hula dancers. This fern is one of the plants which is sacred to Laka, the goddess of hula and the forest. Also called "palai," the fern has a wonderful fragrance that transmits more scent as you wear it.

RIC NOYLE

Maui Calendar of Events

2000

JUNE

1 • MAUI FILM FESTIVAL AT WAILEA – Hawaiian culture meets the Big Screen at the inauguration of this film festival in Wailea Resort, which continues through the 3rd. Film premieres, Opening Night Gala, Filmmakers' Panels, award presentations, Taste of Wailea, Hawaiian music and dance, and guest celebrities. 888-999-6330.

4 • MAUI SYMPHONY ORCHESTRA & FESTIVAL – This Season Festival Finale was formerly known as Maui Chamber Music Festival. World-class soloists of chamber music and Maui's symphony orchestra present a four-concert series featuring the music of Mozart, Faure, Telemann and Vivaldi. Continues through the 11th. 242-7469.

10 • KING KAMEHAMEHA DAY PARADE & HO'OLAULE'A – A colorful float parade through Lahaina features Pa'u riders on horses decorated with exotic island flowers, marching bands, decorated vehicles and walking units all honoring King Kamehameha the Great. A festival is held at Banyan Tree Park with food, crafters, and Hawaiian entertainment. 888-310-1117.
• UPCOUNTRY FAIR – An old-fashioned country fair with livestock auction, farmers market, island product and craft booths, ancestry museum, cooking competition, food booths, and live entertainment. Eddie Tam Memorial Complex in Makawao. 242-2278.

11 • 7TH ANNUAL BANKOH KIHO'ALU GUITAR FEST – Hawaii's top slack key guitarists showcase this traditional art form at the amphitheater of Maui Arts & Cultural Center in Wailuku; 12noon-5:30pm. 242-7469.

RON DAHLQUIST

JULY

1 • O BON SEASON FESTIVAL – Japanese O Bon Season begins when ancestral spirits are invited to join in the harvest. Ceremony begins at 7pm, followed by Floating Lantern ceremony of candle-lit boats. Traditional Japanese dances are performed. Jodo Mission in Lahaina. 661-4304.
• MAKAWAO RODEO & PANIOLO PARADE – Maui Roping Club presents the largest rodeo in Hawai'i with more than 350 cowboys from all over the world. From 1-4pm on 1st and 2nd, watch competitors ride, rope and run for top prizes. Oskie Rice Arena. Paniolo Parade opens the event at 9am along Baldwin Ave. in Makawao Town.
• KAPALUA WINE & FOOD SYMPOSIUM – World-renowned winemakers and Hawaii's hottest chefs are showcased throughout Kapalua Resort in wine tastings, seminars and gourmet dinners, through the 3rd. Includes The Grand Tasting and Chefs Seafood Festival. 800-KAPALUA.
• WAILEA OPEN TENNIS CHAMPIONSHIPS – One of Hawaii's most popular, this 16th annual tennis tourney attracts players from around the world, and continues through the 4th. Competition is in A,B,C,D and Open divisions; men and women; singles and doubles. Wailea Resort, 879-1958.

4 • KAANAPALI BEACH RESORT JULY 4TH CELEBRATION – A wide variety of family fun activities are scheduled all day through the resort, including kids games and face painting, food booths and BBQ, live music along with a huge fireworks display after sunset. 800-245-9229.

AUGUST

4 • MAUI ONION FESTIVAL – Kaanapali pays tribute to the Maui Onion, known worldwide for its sweet, mild flavor, through the 6th. Enjoy farmers market, crafts fair, Professional Chefs demo's, cook-offs, Maui Onion Eating Contest, lots of food and music. Whalers Village, 661-4567.

18 • MAUI CALLS BENEFIT AT MAUI ARTS & CULTURAL CENTER – A return to the enchanting days of 1930s Hawai'i and indulge in the best food and wines found on Maui. 12 chefs present gourmet pupus and 16 vineyards feature fine wine tastings. Hawaiian music and a benefit auction, all in outdoor amphitheater. 242-7469.

SEPTEMBER

1 • MAUI WRITERS CONFERENCE – Held at the Grand Wailea Resort & Spa, this world-renowned event brings top literary agents, editors, authors, columnists and screenwriters to Maui for some major networking. Featured celebrity speakers, evening functions, and seminars for writers. Continues through the 4th. 879-0061.

4 • KAPALUA OPEN TENNIS TOURNAMENT – Hawaii's hottest tennis stars heat up during this annual Labor Day competition. Men's and women's singles and doubles, plus B and C division play, at Kapalua's Tennis Garden and Village Tennis Center. 669-5677.

8 • MAUI CHEFS PRESENT . . . Twelve of the island's most innovative chefs present their best at this dinner and cocktail party under the stars, which kicks-off A Taste of Lahaina. An evening of gourmet food, open bar, entertainment and silent auction. Benefits Maui youth groups. 6:30 to 10pm; 888-310-1117.

9 • A TASTE OF LAHAINA & THE BEST OF ISLAND MUSIC – Maui's largest culinary festival is in its 9th year, showcasing 40 restaurants and their signature dishes, a beer garden, wine tasting, top chefs cooking demo's, huge kids' game zone, and continuous live entertainment on stage with Hawaii's current and legendary musicians. Benefits Maui community groups. Outdoors; 5 to 10 pm, 9th and 10th. 888-310-1117.

22 • KAPALUA'S EARTH MAUI NATURE SUMMIT – Audubon International Conference conservation workshops, Golf in the Environment Tournament at The Bay Course, Pu'u Kukui Nature Walk, and other activities showcasing Hawai'i and its fragile environment at the Kapalua Resort, through the 27th. 800-KAPALUA.

OCTOBER

5 • MAUI COUNTY FAIR – The oldest county fair in the islands (78th annual) boasts carnival rides and games, multi-ethnic food court, live entertainment, horticulture and homemaking exhibits. Continues through the 8th. War Memorial Complex in Wailuku. 871-6230.

6 • ALOHA FESTIVALS ON MAUI – A series of Hawaiian cultural events, including appearances by the Maui Royal Court, community celebrations, arts and craft displays throughout the island, through the 15th. A parade, games, a jamboree and luau take place in Hana. 244-3530.

16 • EMC KAANAPALI CLASSIC SENIOR PGA TOUR – The legends of golf tee it up at Kaanapali's North Course for this popular annual classic, through the 22nd. Includes a 36-hole Pro-Am tournament and 36 holes of professional play. Free admission. 661-1885.

21 • TERRY FOX CANCER RESEARCH BENEFIT – Four Seasons Resort at Wailea hosts this annual fundraiser with a 10K Run/5K Walk, Charity Golf Tournament, and Dinner Gala and Silent Auction with concert. 874-8000.

RON DAHLQUIST

22 • XTERRA WORLD CHAMPIONSHIP – Premiere off-road, extreme multi-sport competition televised on Maui. Featuring an ocean swim, mountain bike ride up Haleakala, and off-round run, it attracts a cross-over field of the world's best triathletes and pro mountain bikers. Begins at 9am in the Wailea Resort. 808-521-4322

31 • HALLOWEEN IN LAHAINA – Celebrated since 1990 as the "Mardi Gras of the Pacific," this is more than just a night on the town in costume, and draws thousands to Front Street, which is closed to vehicle traffic from 4pm to 1am. A children's parade kicks-off the evening; crafters and food booths, live music and dancing. The Great Halloween Costume Contest at Banyan Tree Park begins at 7pm. 888-310-1117.

NOVEMBER

11 • HULA O NA KEIKI – Maui's only children's solo hula competition is hosted at the Ka'anapali Beach Hotel. Workshops, arts and crafts displays, and wonderful entertainment, through the 12th. 661-0011.

20 • MAUI INVITATIONAL BASKETBALL TOURNAMENT – Hawaii's Chaminade University hosts NCAA-sanctioned top college teams in this annual pre-season tournament at the Lahaina Civic Center, through the 22nd. 244-3530

RON DAHLQUIST

26 • SENIOR SKINS GAME – Making its inaugural appearance at the Wailea Golf Club, this golf tournament features four of the world's most admired Senior PGA pros playing for two days on Wailea's Gold Course. Continues through the 28th. 800-332-1614.

FEBRUARY

2 • CHINESE NEW YEAR – LahainaTown celebrates with colorful lion dances at the Wo Hing Temple on Front Street. The 800 block of Front Street is closed to vehicle traffic to showcase Chinese martial arts, ethnic foods and traditional music with drums, gongs and cymbals; firecrackers are set-off every hour. 6 to 9pm. 888-310-1117.

17 • WHALE WEEK ON MAUI & WHALE DAY – Maui's longest-running celebration honoring the Humpback whales features special events and kids activities in Kihei, sponsored by Pacific Whale Foundation. Run for the Whales, Parade of Whales, Whale Regatta and more. Week builds up to a 10am-7pm festival on 24th. 879-8860.

MARCH

• ART MAUI – Maui's most popular multi-media exhibit of local artists, and one of the most respected juried exhibits in the state; founded 23 years ago. Runs for four weeks at Maui Arts & Cultural Center's International Gallery. 242-7469

17 • WHALEFEST – Lahaina celebrates the annual migration of Humpback Whales with special guest Jean Michel Cousteau, who leads whale watch, sailing, and diving tours, through the 24th. Ocean Arts Festival, marine lectures with slide shows, beachside dinner with Cousteau films. 888-310-1117.

18 • MAUI MARATHON – Aptly billed as "Run with the Whales," this 26.2-mile course from Kahului to Kaanapali is recognized as one of the 10 most scenic marathons in the nation. Entries from an international field are up to 2500 runners. Carbo-load parties and a Fitness Expo precede over the weekend. 871-6441

APRIL

14 • DAVID MALO DAY – Cultural performances with Hawaiian music and hula honor the life of Hawaii's famous scholar at Lahainaluna High School. 5pm. 662-4000.

21 • BANYAN TREE BIRTHDAY PARTY – The 128th birthday of LahainaTown's famous Banyan Tree is celebrated with a birthday cake, artists displaying nature artworks, and hands-on art activities for children to portray the tree. Continues through 22nd. 9am to 5pm. 888-310-1117.

DECEMBER

1 • FESTIVAL OF ART & FLOWERS & LIGHTING OF THE BANYAN TREE – The historic Banyan Tree in Lahaina is lit up for the holiday season on opening night. Students sing Christmas carols in Hawaiian, accompanied by senior ukulele players. Festival of Art & Flowers, along with original art and fine crafts from Maui artists. Held at Old Lahaina Courthouse; includes floral arranging and decorating workshops, artists-in-action, and music. Continues through the 3rd. 888-310-1117.

8 • NA MELE O MAUI – Children's celebration of the Hawaiian culture through music, singing and art. Over 1,000 Maui County students sing traditional songs in the Hawaiian language in a competition by age group. Held in Kaanapali Resort. High school students exhibit their art works. 800-245-9229.

2001

JANUARY

4 • MERCEDES CHAMPIONSHIPS – PGA TOUR winners from 2000 compete in the season-opening golf tournament at Kapalua's Plantation Course for a record $3,000,000 purse. Portion of the proceeds benefit Maui charities. Last year's champion-of-the-champions was Tiger Woods. Continues through the 7th. 888-310-GOLF.

20 • HULA BOWL MAUI – This collegiate all-star football classic is in its 4th year on Maui; it's the 55th anniversary of the game. Held at the War Memorial Stadium in Wailuku; kick-off at 11am. Special activities and autograph signings precede the game during Hulafest Week (15-19). 244-3530

MAY

1 • **MAY DAY IS LEI DAY** – Throughout Hawai'i, May 1st means making, wearing and sharing leis. Outrigger Wailea Resort hosts a fun-filled day of lei displays and competition, Hawaiian entertainment, food and activities. 879-1922.

12 • **SEABURY HALL CRAFTS FAIR** – An annual fundraiser of island crafts, art demonstrations, kids activities with pony rides, and entertainment at Maui's scenic private high school on Olina Road above Makawao. 572-7235.

19 • **IN CELEBRATION OF CANOES** – Maui's Signature Cultural Event of Hawaii's heritage honors the voyaging canoe which united all of Polynesia. Continues through the 31st. Master carvers from Pacific islands create canoes from wood logs throughout in LahainaTown. Enjoy a traditional welcome ceremony and closing lu'au feast, cultural arts demo's, and Festival of Canoes & Parade (25th) featuring warrior performances, crafts, food, and an outdoor concert with Hawaii's top musicians. 888-310-1117.

26 • **MAUI MUSIC FESTIVAL** – The best in Adult Contemporary Jazz is featured day and night throughout Kaanapali Resort with world-renowned musicians on stage, through the 27th. Food booths on the Kaanapali Golf Course and an After-Hours Jam at hotels. 800-628-4767.

ONGOING EVENTS

• Maui is world-renowned for its surfing spots and windsurfing beaches. Throughout the year, there are many pro and amateur surfing competitions in all ages and classes, as well as wavesailing classics and windsurfing races. Contact the Maui Visitors Bureau, 808-244-3530 or www.visitmaui.com.

• Visiting Artists and Artists-in-Residence Programs are popular at Maui's world-class resorts. Watch Maui's artists in action at The Ritz-Carlton, Kapalua and Four Seasons Maui at Wailea. On the island of Lana'i, distinguished authors, musicians, artists and filmmakers give lectures at The Manele Bay Hotel and The Lodge at Koele. The Kea Lani Hotel in Wailea hosts a series of Food & Wine Masters, featuring renowned Chef demonstrations, signature dinners and wine pairings.

• Art and More! Maui has also become known as an art capital. Friday Night is Art Night in LahainaTown, every Friday from 7-10pm. Stroll the galleries along Front Street and its environs and enjoy special showings, artist demo's, and pupu receptions. Makawao has been named one of the Top U.S. Arts travel destinations. This picturesque Upcountry "cowboy" town has a wide variety of fine art galleries and local craft boutiques.

Ongoing arts fairs include the He U'i Cultural Arts Festival every 1st and 3rd weekend under the Banyan Tree in Lahaina, as well as the Lahaina Arts Society Craft Fair held every 2nd and 4th weekend. Also, be sure to visit the Maui Arts & Cultural Center, Maui's premier performing and fine arts complex in Wailuku. World-class art exhibits are showcased in the Schaefer International Gallery, changing monthly. The Ho'onaunea Hou music series features Hawaii's best musical artists in concert at its state-of-the-art Castle Theater, which is also home to the Maui Film Festival, offering outstanding contemporary films every Wednesday.

RON DAHLQUIST

MAUI COUNTY FACTS

Nickname: The Valley Isle
County Flower: Lokelani (heavenly rose)
Size: 728.6 square miles (second largest island in Hawaii)
Population: Approximately 100,000 permanent residents (third largest island population in Hawaii)
Visitors: More than 2.4 million a year (second largest among the Hawaiian Islands); the "de facto" population (number of visitors and residents at any one time) is approximately 135,000.
Politics: Maui County includes the islands of Maui, Molokai, Lanai and Kaho'olawe (uninhabited) with a total population of about 108,000. It is governed by a separately elected mayor and 9-member county council. There are no city, township or borough governments. The seat of government in Maui County is located in Wailuku.
Geography: Maui is located at approximately 21° north of the equator in a small island group that is the most isolated land in the world. The nearest land mass to Hawaii is San Francisco, approximately 2,400 miles away. Of the total of more than 100 islands in Hawaii, eight are considered major islands—Ni'ihau, Kauai, Oahu, Molokai, Maui, Lanai, Kaho'olawe, and the Big Island of Hawaii — only seven are inhabited. Maui has no navigatable rivers, but there are hundreds of streams. The only natural body of water is the 40-acre Kanaha Pond, a major bird sanctuary near the airport in Kahului.
Highest Peaks: Puu Ulaula at the summit of Haleakala, 10,023 feet; second highest is Puu Kukui in the West Maui mountains, 5,788 feet.

CLIMATE

Hawaii's temperature is usually a sunny, comfortable mid-70 to mid-80 degrees with two mildly discernible seasons – winter and summer.

The summer months are normally warmer and sometimes muggy due to moderate to low trade winds. Days are longer with sunrise at around 5:44am and sunset at around 7:03pm.

The start of winter season means slightly cooler mornings and evenings from late October to early April. Days are shorter. Sunrise is around 6:46am and the sun sets at around 5:44pm. Trade winds range from moderate to gusty.

Ocean temperatures average about 75° during mornings in March and about 77° in the afternoon; August water temperatures average about 78° in the morning and 82° in the afternoon. Tides are moderate, averaging usually about two feet.

Hawaiian winds normally blow from the northeast and bring fair weather. But when the winds shift to blow from the south, they are called Kona winds and often bring storms in the winter.

HAWAII STATE FACTS

Statehood: Hawaii was made the 50th state in the United States in 1959; **Nickname:** "The Aloha State"; **Motto:** "The Life of the Land is Perpetuated in Righteousness"; **State Flower:** Hibiscus; **State Tree:** Kukui, or Candlenut Tree; **State Bird:** Nene, or Hawaiian Goose; **State Mammal:** Humpback Whale

GOOD NUMBERS TO KNOW

The area code for the state of Hawaii is (808).
To dial to other islands you must dial 1-808 before the number.

- Emergencies—Dial 911 (Ambulance, fire, police departments). An emergency number from any phone booth. No coins are needed to dial.
- Better Business Bureau 1-808-536-6956
- Poison Center 1-800-362-3585
- Telephone Assistance 1-411
  Inter-island 1-808-555-1212
  Mainland .1-area code-555-1212
- Time of day 242-0212
- Weather Forecast, Maui 877-5111
- Maui Visitors Bureau 871-8691
- Haelakala National Park .572-7749

Directory of Advertisers

PIONEER

LAHAINA
Restoration Foundation
HISTORIC SITE

The
PIONEER INN
8